Red Line **1**

Vokabeltraining aktiv

Herausgeber: Dr. Frank Haß

Ernst Klett Verlag
Stuttgart • Leipzig

Liebe Schülerinnen und Schüler,

mit *Vokabeltraining aktiv* kannst du alle neuen Vokabeln aus Red Line 1 üben.

Auf jeder Seite findest du einen Kasten mit dem Titel „What's the word?", wo du die Lücken vervollständigen kannst.

What's the word?

Auf Wiedersehen, Jonas.   *Goodbye* , Jonas .

boy

weiß ⟷ schwarz   white ⟷ black

Sieh dir die Beispiele im Kasten an. Hier musst du z. B.
- den deutschen Satz links übersetzen und hierfür das unterstrichene Wort auf Englisch einsetzen
- den englischen Begriff für das Bild einsetzen.

Wenn das Zeichen ⟷ auftaucht, dann ist das Gegenteil gesucht.

Wir haben uns auch viele Rätsel und spannende Übungen für dich ausgedacht. Diese findest du immer auf der unteren Hälfte jeder Seite.

Unter der Überschrift *Blue words* findest du alle blau gedruckten Wörter deines Englischbuchs einer *Unit* zusammengefasst.

Hier sind noch einige Tipps, wie du die neuen Vokabeln aus Red Line 1 mit *Vokabeltraining aktiv* üben kannst:
- Vervollständige die Lücken mit Bleistift, so kannst du dich jederzeit korrigieren.
- Deine Lösungen kannst du im Lösungsheft selbst überprüfen.
- Achte immer auf die korrekte Schreibung der Wörter.
- Notiere die Wörter, bei denen du Schwierigkeiten hattest, und lerne sie besonders sorgfältig, z. B. mit Karteikarten. Versuche später noch einmal, die Sätze zu vervollständigen.
- Wenn du alle wichtigen Wörter einer Seite gut gelernt hast, kannst du versuchen, die englischen Übungssätze abzudecken und die deutschen still zu übersetzen.

Nun wünschen wir dir viel Spaß und Erfolg mit *Vokabeltraining aktiv*!

Dein *Red Line* Team

What's the word?

1. Hi. Ich bin Jonas.

    _____ . _____ Jonas.

2. Wie heißt du?

    _____ ?

3. Hallo! Ich heiße Elena.

    _____ ! _____ Elena.

4. Nett, dich kennen zu lernen.

    _____ .

5. Es ist Zeit, zu gehen.

    _____ .

6. Auf Wiedersehen, Jonas.

    _____ , Jonas.

7. Tschüss und bis bald, Elena.

    _____ , Elena.

1 Put in the right words. Setze die richtigen Wörter ein.

1. Hello. _____ Elena.

2. What's _____ name?

3. My name _____ Jonas.

4. Nice to _____ you.

5. It's time _____ go.

6. See you _____ , Elena.

to	meet
I'm	your
later	is

2 Complete the crossword. Vervollständige das Kreuzworträtsel.

Down ▼ :

1. Jonas: Hi! My … is Jonas!

2. Jonas: What's … name?

Across ▶ :

3. Elena: … I'm Elena.

4. Elena: Nice to … you.

Down ▼ :

5. Jonas: It's … to go.

6. Jonas: See you … .

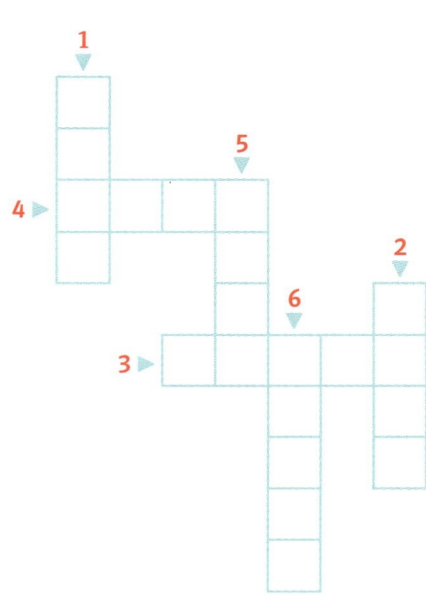

What's the word?

1. Willkommen – Hallo! _____ – Hello!
2. Grüß dich. _____ .
3. Ich mag Musik. I like _____ .
4. Ich mag Englisch. _____ .
5.  _____
6. Ich mag Tiere. Und du? I like _____ . _____ ?
7. Ja, ich mag Ben die Fledermaus. _____ , I like Ben _____ .
8. Ich mag Sport. I like _____ .
9. Es ist Zeit zu gehen. Tschüss. It's time to go. _____ .

3 Write the words. Finde die Wörter und schreibe sie auf Englisch und Deutsch auf.

1. eWeolmc. _____
2. Geoybdo. _____
3. eSe ouy trale. _____
4. lleoH rehet. _____

4 Look at the pictures and write the words. Schau dir die Bilder an und schreibe die Wörter auf.

I like ❶ _____ . I like ❸ _____ . I like ❺ _____ .
I like ❷ _____ . I like ❹ _____ .

5 Put a circle around the wrong number and write the word. Welche Zahl ist falsch?
Kreise sie ein und schreibe sie als Wort auf.

a) 1 • 3 • 6 • 9 _____   c) 8 • 5 • 4 • 3 • 2 _____   e) 10 • 9 • 8 • 4 • 7 • 6 _____
b) 1 • 2 • 3 • 4 • 9 _____   d) 1 • 3 • 5 • 0 • 7 _____   f) 2 • 4 • 6 • 7 • 8 • 10 _____

What's the word?

1. _____

2. Drei ist eine Zahl.   Three is a _____ .

3. Ich kann einen Fußball kaufen.   _____ a football.

4. Ich kann Tennis spielen.   I can play _____ .

5. Ich mag Aktivitäten.   I like _____ .

6. Ich kann Fußball spielen.   _____ .

7. Ich kann in einem Park spielen.   I can play _____ a _____ .

8. Ich sehe was, was du nicht siehst …   _____

9.   _____

10. Es ist etwas Schwarzes.   It's _____ black.

11. Orange ist eine Farbe.   Orange is a _____ .

6 Look at the picture – right or wrong? Tick ✔ the right box.

Was siehst du auf dem Bild auf Seite 10/11 im Buch? Sind die Sätze richtig oder falsch? Kreuze ✔ an.

In the park …	right	wrong
I can spy a boy.	☐	☐
I can spy a bus.	☐	☐
I can spy two cats.	☐	☐
I can spy a bat.	☐	☐
I can spy three dogs.	☐	☐
I can spy a football.	☐	☐
I can spy two numbers.	☐	☐
I can spy people.	☐	☐

7 Complete the words. Vervollständige die Wörter mit den fehlenden Buchstaben.

A A A E E E E E E I I I I O O O

1. n _ mb _ r   4. p _ _ _ pl _   7. _ ct _ v _ ty   O O O

2. s _ m _ th _ ng   5. b _ y   8. c _ l _ _ r   U U

3. p _ r k   6. t _ nn _ s   9. _ r _ ng _

What's the word?

1. Es ist ein Bus. _____ a _____ .

2. Der Bus ist grün. The bus is _____ .

3. Ich mag Hunde. I like _____ .

4. Der Hund ist braun und weiß. The dog is _____ and _____ .

5. Der Fußball ist gelb. The football is _____ .

6. weiß ⟷ schwarz. white ⟷ _____ .

7.  _____

8. Ich mag orange, blau und rot. I like _____ and _____ .

9. Es ist eine Fledermaus. It's _____ bat.

10. Die Fledermaus ist hier. _____ bat is _____ .

8 Find the colours. Write the English and German words.

Finde die Farben. Schreibe sie auf Englisch und Deutsch auf.

_____ _____ _____ _____

_____ _____ _____ _____

_____ _____ _____

9 Look at the pictures and complete the sentences. Schau dir die Bilder an und vervollständige die Sätze.

1. Ben is _____ .   3. The dog is _____ .   5. The bus is _____ .

2. The cat is _____ .   4. My computer is _____ .   6. The football is _____ .

What's the word?

1. Dies ist ein Foto.   _____ is a _____ .

2.

    _____

3.

    _____

4.

    _____

5. Ein Hund ist ein Haustier.   A dog is a _____ .

6. Woher kommst du?   _____ ?

7. Ich komme aus Deutschland.   _____ .

8. Er kommt aus England.   _____ .

9. Wie alt bist du?   _____ ?

10. Ich bin zwölf. Und du?   I'm _____ . And you?

11. Ich bin elf.   I'm _____ .

1 Find ten words.

a) Find the English words. (↓ and →) Finde die englischen Wörter.

A	S	D	F	G	C	A	T	O
P	E	T	R	U	L	I	W	D
T	L	D	B	I	K	E	E	O
V	E	D	Z	N	Y	X	L	G
B	V	S	D	E	L	M	V	Z
G	E	R	M	A	N	Y	E	U
E	N	Z	R	P	H	O	T	O
F	F	T	H	I	S	I	O	P
C	B	F	L	G	D	K	D	S

b) Write the words. Schreibe die Wörter auf.

Meerschweinchen _____   zwölf _____

Deutschland _____   Fahrrad _____

Foto _____   dies _____

Haustier _____   elf _____

Hund _____   Katze _____

What's the word?

1. Mein Name ist Luke.

    _____ name is Luke.

2. Ich bin Fußballfan.

    I'm a _____ .

3. Mein Meerschweinchen Luis ist verrückt.

    My guinea pig Luis is _____ .

4. Meine Glückszahl ist die sieben.

    My _____ is seven.

5. Das ist mein Haustier.

    _____ my pet.

6. Er ist ein Junge.

    _____ a boy.

7. Sie sind cool.

    _____ .

2 **Put in the right words.** Setze die richtigen Wörter ein.

| That's | That's | crazy | lucky number | He's | My | fan |

Hi! I'm Luke. I'm eleven. This is my pet,
Sherlock. _____ a crazy dog.
1

Hi! _____ name is Holly.
I'm a tennis _____ .
_____ my pet.
It's a guinea pig. It's _____ .
2

Hello! I'm Olivia.
My _____ is four.
I'm from Greenwich.
_____ in England.
3

3 **Put a circle around the right word.** Kreise das richtige Wort ein.

1. That's (my • he's) friend.

2. He's (lucky number • crazy).

3. (My • That's) a football.

4. My friend is a football (cool • fan).

5. My lucky (fan • number) is ten.

6. This is Luke. (My • He's) cool.

What's the word?

1. Ich habe zwei Schwestern.

I have two _____ .

2. Aber ich habe keine Brüder. Und du?

_____ I have _____ . And you?

3. Ich habe einen Bruder.

I have one _____ .

4. Das ist unser Computer.

This is _____ computer.

5. Ich lese Hollys E-Mail.

I read Holly's _____ .

6. Ich habe einen Hund. Er ist mein Freund.

_____ a dog. He's my _____ .

7. Sein Name ist Luke.

_____ is Luke.

8. Das ist ein Foto von Luke.

This is a photo _____ Luke.

9. Meine Mutter kommt aus Greenwich.

My _____ is from Greenwich.

10. Mein Vater kommt aus Deutschland.

My _____ is from Germany.

11. Ich mag meinen Papa und meine Mama.

I like my _____ and my _____ .

4 Put a circle around the odd one out. Welches Wort passt nicht in die Reihe? Kreise es ein.

1. father • sister • brother • friend

2. ten • eleven • one • but

3. dad • black • purple • red

4. his • of • our • her

5. he's • she's • it's • I have

6. brother • cat • guinea pig • dog

5 Look at the picture and write the words. Schau dir das Bild an und schreibe die Wörter auf.

1 _____

2 _____

3 _____

4 _____

5 _____

6 _____

What's the word?

1. Ich bin hier mit meiner Familie.

   I'm here_____ my _____ .

2. Wir sind im Garten.

   _____ in the_____ .

3. Meine Freundin auch.

   My friend _____ .

4. Sie ist nett.

   _____ .

5. Ich mag sie.

   I like _____ .

6. Das ist ein Familienfoto. Ich bin neben meiner Mutter.

   This is a family photo. I'm _____ my mum.

7. Meine Freundin ist neben mir.

   My friend is next to _____ .

8. Du bist auch meine Freundin.

   _____ my friend too.

6 Find the words. Write the English and German words.
Finde die Wörter. Schreibe sie auf Englisch und Deutsch auf.

we'rewithfamilyhergardennexttotooyou're

_____   _____

_____   _____

_____   _____

_____   _____

7 Write the long form. Schreibe die Wörter in der Langform aus.

1. I'm _____

2. they're _____

3. you're _____

4. it's _____

5. she's _____

6. he's _____

Red Line **1**

Vokabeltraining aktiv

Lösungsheft

What's the word?

1. Hi. Ich bin Jonas.   _Hi_ _____ . I'm _____ Jonas.

2. Wie heißt du?   _What's your name_ _____ ?

3. Hallo! Ich heiße Elena.   _Hello_ _____ ! _My name is_ _____ Elena.

4. Nett, dich kennen zu lernen.   _Nice to meet you_ _____

5. Es ist Zeit, zu gehen.   _It's time to go_ _____ .

6. Auf Wiedersehen, Jonas.   _Goodbye_ _____ , Jonas.

7. Tschüss und bis bald, Elena.   _See you later_ _____ , Elena.

1 Put in the right words. Setze die richtigen Wörter ein.

1. Hello. _I'm_ Elena.

2. What's _your_ name?

3. My name _is_ Jonas.

4. Nice to _meet_ you.

5. It's time _to_ go.

6. See you _later_ , Elena.

to	meet
I'm	your
later	is

2 Complete the crossword. Vervollständige das Kreuzworträtsel.

Down ▼ :

1. Jonas: Hi! My ... is Jonas!

2. Jonas: What's ... name?

Across ▶ :

3. Elena: ... I'm Elena.

4. Elena: Nice to ... you.

Down ▼ :

5. Jonas: It's ... to go.

6. Jonas: See you ... .

```
                    1
                    N
          5
          A
  4▶ M E E T
          E     I
                M     2
              6       Y
        3▶ H E L L O
                A     U
                T     R
                E
                R
```

What's the word?

1. Willkommen – Hallo!   _Welcome_ – Hello!

2. Grüß dich.   _Hello there_ .

3. Ich mag Musik.   I like _music_ .

4. Ich mag Englisch.   I like _English_ .

5.   _computer_

6. Ich mag Tiere. Und du?   I like _animals_ . _And you_ ?

7. Ja, ich mag Ben die Fledermaus.   _Yes_ , I like Ben _the bat_ .

8. Ich mag Sport.   I like _sport_ .

9. Es ist Zeit zu gehen. Tschüss.   It's time to go. _Bye_ .

3 Write the words. Finde die Wörter und schreibe sie auf Englisch und Deutsch auf.

1. eWeolmc. _Welcome. – Willkommen._

2. Geoybdo. _Goodbye. – Auf Wiedersehen._

3. eSe ouy trale. _See you later. – Tschüss.; Bis bald._

4. lleoH rehet. _Hello there. – Hallo.; Grüß dich._

4 Look at the pictures and write the words. Schau dir die Bilder an und schreibe die Wörter auf.

I like ❶ _computers_ .   I like ❸ _animals_ .   I like ❺ _English_ .

I like ❷ _music_ .   I like ❹ _sport_ .

5 Put a circle around the wrong number and write the word. Welche Zahl ist falsch?
Kreise sie ein und schreibe sie als Wort auf.

a) ①•3•6•9   _one_   c) ⑧•5•4•3•2   _eight_   e) 10•9•8•④•7•6   _four_

b) 1•2•3•4•⑨   _nine_   d) 1•3•5•⓪•7   _zero_   f) 2•4•6•⑦•8•10   _seven_

What's the word?

1.   _boy_

2. Drei ist eine Zahl.   Three is a _number_ .

3. Ich kann einen Fußball kaufen. _I can buy_ a football.

4. Ich kann Tennis spielen.   I can play _tennis_ .

5. Ich mag Aktivitäten.   I like _activities_ .

6. Ich kann Fußball spielen.   _I can play football_ .

7. Ich kann in einem Park spielen. I can play _in_ a _park_ .

8. Ich sehe was, was du nicht siehst ... _I spy with my little eye ..._

9.   _people_

10. Es ist etwas Schwarzes.   It's _something_ black.

11. Orange ist eine Farbe.   Orange is a _colour_ .

6 Look at the picture – right or wrong? Tick ✔ the right box.
Was siehst du auf dem Bild auf Seite 10/11 im Buch? Sind die Sätze richtig oder falsch? Kreuze ✔ an.

In the park ...	right	wrong
I can spy a boy.	✔	☐
I can spy a bus.	✔	☐
I can spy two cats.	☐	✔
I can spy a bat.	☐	✔
I can spy three dogs.	☐	✔
I can spy a football.	✔	☐
I can spy two numbers.	✔	☐
I can spy people.	✔	☐

7 Complete the words. Vervollständige die Wörter mit den fehlenden Buchstaben.

A A A E E E E E E I I I I O O O

1. n u m b e r
2. s o m e t h i n g
3. p a r k
4. p e o p l e
5. b o y
6. t e n n i s
7. a c t i v i t y   O O O
8. c o l o u r
9. o r a n g e   U U

What's the word?

1. Es ist ein Bus. — It's ___ a bus ___ .
2. Der Bus ist grün. — The bus is green ___ .
3. Ich mag Hunde. — I like dogs ___ .
4. Der Hund ist braun und weiß. — The dog is brown ___ and white ___ .
5. Der Fußball ist gelb. — The football is yellow ___ .
6. weiß ⟷ schwarz. — white ⟷ black ___ .
7. 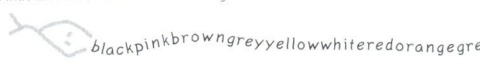 — purple ___
8. Ich mag orange, blau und rot. — I like orange, blue ___ and red ___ .
9. Es ist eine Fledermaus. — It's a ___ bat.
10. Die Fledermaus ist hier. — The ___ bat is here ___ .

8 Find the colours. Write the English and German words.
Finde die Farben. Schreibe sie auf Englisch und Deutsch auf.

blackpinkbrowngreyyellowwhiteredorangegreenpurpleblue

black – schwarz   pink – pink   brown – braun   grey – grau
yellow – gelb   white – weiss   red – rot   orange – orange
green – grün   purple – lila   blue – blau

9 Look at the pictures and complete the sentences. Schau dir die Bilder an und vervollständige die Sätze.

1. Ben is brown ___ .
3. The dog is pink ___ .
5. The bus is red ___ .

2. The cat is white ___ .
4. My computer is black ___ .
6. The football is blue ___ .

What's the word?

1. Dies ist ein Foto. — This ___ is a photo ___ .
2. [Bild] — guinea pig ___
3. [Bild Fahrrad] — bike ___
4. [Bild Katze] — cat ___
5. Ein Hund ist ein Haustier. — A dog is a pet ___ .
6. Woher kommst du? — Where are you from ___ ?
7. Ich komme aus Deutschland. — I'm from Germany ___
8. Er kommt aus England. — He's from England ___ .
9. Wie alt bist du? — How old are you ___ ?
10. Ich bin zwölf. Und du? — I'm twelve ___ . And you?
11. Ich bin elf. — I'm eleven ___ .

1 Find ten words.

a) Find the English words. (↓ and →) Finde die englischen Wörter.

A	S	D	F	G	C	A	T	O
P	E	T	R	U	L	I	W	D
T	L	D	B	I	K	E	E	O
V	E	D	Z	N	Y	X	L	G
B	V	S	D	E	L	M	S	M
G	E	R	M	A	N	Y	E	U
E	N	Z	R	P	H	O	T	O
F	F	T	H	I	S	I	O	P
C	B	F	L	G	D	K	D	S

b) Write the words. Schreibe die Wörter auf.

Meerschweinchen guinea pig   zwölf twelve
Deutschland Germany   Fahrrad bike
Foto photo   dies this
Haustier pet   elf eleven
Hund dog   Katze cat

What's the word?

1. Mein Name ist Luke. — My ___ name is Luke.
2. Ich bin Fußballfan. — I'm a football fan ___ .
3. Mein Meerschweinchen Luis ist verrückt. — My guinea pig Luis is crazy ___ .
4. Meine Glückszahl ist die sieben. — My lucky number ___ is seven.
5. Das ist mein Haustier. — That's ___ my pet.
6. Er ist ein Junge. — He's ___ a boy.
7. Sie sind cool. — They're cool ___ .

2 Put in the right words. Setze die richtigen Wörter ein.

[That's] [That's] [crazy] [lucky number] [He's] [My] [fan]

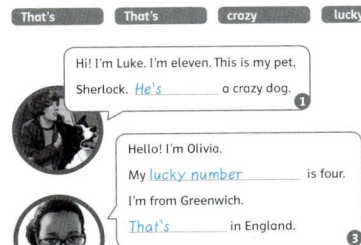
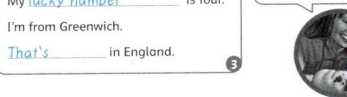

Hi! I'm Luke. I'm eleven. This is my pet,
Sherlock. He's ___ a crazy dog. ①

Hi! My ___ name is Holly.
I'm a tennis fan ___ .
That's ___ my pet.
It's a guinea pig. It's crazy ___ ②

Hello! I'm Olivia.
My lucky number ___ is four.
I'm from Greenwich.
That's ___ in England. ③

3 Put a circle around the right word. Kreise das richtige Wort ein.

1. That's (my) • he's) friend.
2. He's (lucky number • crazy).
3. (My • That's) a football.
4. My friend is a football (cool • fan).
5. My lucky (fan • number) is ten.
6. This is Luke. (My • He's) cool.

What's the word?

1. Ich habe zwei Schwestern. — I have two sisters ___ .
2. Aber ich habe keine Brüder. Und du? — But ___ I have no brothers ___ . And you?
3. Ich habe einen Bruder. — I have one brother ___ .
4. Das ist unser Computer. — This is our ___ computer.
5. Ich lese Hollys E-Mail. — I read Holly's e-mail ___ .
6. Ich habe einen Hund. Er ist mein Freund. — I have ___ a dog. He's my friend ___ .
7. Sein Name ist Luke. — His name ___ is Luke.
8. Das ist ein Foto von Luke. — This is a photo of ___ Luke.
9. Meine Mutter kommt aus Greenwich. — My mother ___ is from Greenwich.
10. Mein Vater kommt aus Deutschland. — My father ___ is from Germany.
11. Ich mag meinen Papa und meine Mama. — I like my dad ___ and my mum ___ .

4 Put a circle around the odd one out. Welches Wort passt nicht in die Reihe? Kreise es ein.

1. father • sister • brother • (friend)
2. ten • eleven • one • (but)
3. (dad) • black • purple • red
4. his • (of) • our • her
5. he's • she's • it's • (I have)
6. (brother) • cat • guinea pig • dog

5 Look at the picture and write the words. Schau dir das Bild an und schreibe die Wörter auf.

① mum / mother ___
② dad / father ___
③ sister ___
④ (two) brothers ___
⑤ cat ___
⑥ dog ___

What's the word?

1. Ich bin hier mit meiner Familie. — I'm here with my family .
2. Wir sind im Garten. — We're in the garden .
3. Meine Freundin auch. — My friend too .
4. Sie ist nett. — She's nice .
5. Ich mag sie. — I like her .
6. Das ist ein Familienfoto. Ich bin neben meiner Mutter. — This is a family photo. I'm next to my mum.
7. Meine Freundin ist neben mir. — My friend is next to me .
8. Du bist auch meine Freundin. — You're my friend too.

6 Find the words. Write the English and German words.
Finde die Wörter. Schreibe sie auf Englisch und Deutsch auf.

we'rewithfamilyhergardennexttotooyou're

we're – wir sind   with – mit
family – Familie   her – sie
garden – Garten   next to – neben
too – auch   you're – du bist

7 Write the long form. Schreibe die Wörter in der Langform aus.

1. I'm I am   4. it's it is
2. they're they are   5. she's she is
3. you're you are   6. he's he is

What's the word?

1. Das ist mein Schlafzimmer. — This is my bedroom .
2. Ich habe einen 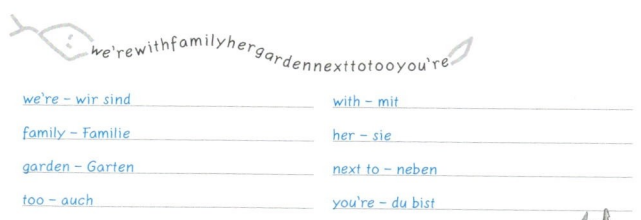 — I have a table .
3. Das ist ein schönes Poster. — This is a nice poster .
4. Der Fußball ist auf dem Bett. — The football is on the bed .
5. Ich habe einen — I have a chair .
6. Das ist eine Kiste. — This is a box .
7. Das Buch ist auf dem Regal. — The book is on the shelf .
8. Mein Handy ist schwarz. — My mobile is black.
9. Lukes T-Shirt ist blau. — Luke's T-shirt is blue.

8 Write the words. Finde die Wörter und schreibe sie auf.

1. beoomrd bedroom   6. tlabe table
2. potsre poster   7. miloeb heonp mobile phone
3. xbo box   8. T-ritsh T-shirt
4. cairh chair   9. shesvel shelves
5. kobo book   10. deb bed

9 Look at the picture and write the words. Schau dir das Bild an und schreibe die Wörter auf.

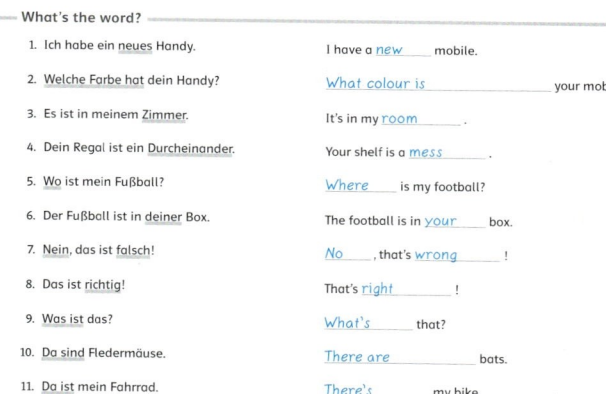

1 bed
2 poster
3 box
4 chair
5 book
6 table
7 mobile phone
8 T-shirt
9 shelf
10 computer

What's the word?

1. Es ist Samstag. — It's Saturday .
2. Ich bin zu Hause. — I'm at home .
3. Wer ist das? — Who is it?
4. Ich bin es! — It's me !
5. Bist du bereit? — Are you ready ?
6. Ich kann meinen Fußball nicht finden. — I can't find my football.
7. Er ist unter dem Bett. — It's under the bed.
8. Wir sind zu spät. — We're late .

10 Write the words in English and German. Schreibe die Wörter auf Englisch und Deutsch auf.

1. er he   5. they sie
2. es it   6. she sie
3. wir wir   7. you du
4. ihr you   8. I ich

11 Put in the right words. Setze die richtigen Wörter ein.

late   at   It's   find   you   under   Who

1. I'm at home.
2. I can't find my football.
3. My dog is under the table.
4. Who is it?
5. We're late .
6. Are you ready?
7. It's Saturday.

What's the word?

1. Ich habe ein neues Handy. — I have a new mobile.
2. Welche Farbe hat dein Handy? — What colour is your mobile?
3. Es ist in meinem Zimmer. — It's in my room .
4. Dein Regal ist ein Durcheinander. — Your shelf is a mess .
5. Wo ist mein Fußball? — Where is my football?
6. Der Fußball ist in deiner Box. — The football is in your box.
7. Nein, das ist falsch! — No , that's wrong !
8. Das ist richtig! — That's right !
9. Was ist das? — What's that?
10. Da sind Fledermäuse. — There are bats.
11. Da ist mein Fahrrad. — There's my bike.

12 Put in the right words. Setze die richtigen Wörter ein.

Sally   Janet

"This is my new mobile."   → "Cool!"
"Where is your mobile?"   → "It's in my room ."
"What colour is your T-shirt?" → "It's green."
"Your room is a mess !"   → "No, no! That's wrong !"
"What's that? A poster?"   → "Yes, that's right ."
"There are cats on your poster." → "Yes, and there's a dog too."

wrong
There
right
colour
new
room
Where
mess
there's
What's

13 Complete the words. Vervollständige die Wörter mit den fehlenden Buchstaben.

A A A E E E E E E E E E I O O O

1. room   4. right   7. mess   10. what's
2. wrong   5. football   8. where   11. there are
3. who   6. new   9. your   12. there's

O O O
O U

What's the word?

1. In unserem Garten gibt es einen Baum. There's a _tree_ in our garden.
2. Meine Mutter ist im Haus. My mother is in the _house_ .
3. Sie ist beschäftigt. She is _busy_ .
4. Später spiele ich Fußball. _Later_ I play football.
5. Ich habe einen merkwürdigen Traum. I have a _funny dream_ .
7.  _night_
8. Niemand ist hier, und es gibt kein Geräusch. _No one_ is here, and there's no _noise_ .
9. Dann spielen wir Fußball. _Then_ we play football.
10. _ladder_
11. _wind_

14 Find ten words.

a) Find the English words. (↓ and →) Finde die englischen Wörter.

B	D	N	T	H	O	U	S	E	G
U	R	I	G	H	T	T	H	E	N
S	V	G	G	H	L	R	B	C	V
Y	B	H	Y	D	R	E	A	M	K
L	A	T	E	R	G	E	H	J	A
G	N	O	O	N	E	D	S	B	S
A	P	I	F	U	N	N	Y	J	D

b) Write the words. Schreibe die Wörter auf.

1. richtig _right_   6. Nacht _night_
2. später _later_   7. Baum _tree_
3. beschäftigt _busy_   8. Traum _dream_
4. Haus _house_   9. merkwürdig _funny_
5. niemand _no one_   10. danach _then_

15 Write the words. Finde die Wörter und schreibe sie auf.

1. dadrel _ladder_   3. diwn _wind_
2. usohe _house_   4. ysbu _busy_

What's the word?

1. zu Hause _around the house_
2. Ich kann meine Katze nicht finden. Na ja, schau mal im Garten nach. I can't find my cat. _Well, look_ in the garden.
3. Danke. _Thanks_ .
4. Meine Mutter ist in der Küche. My mother is in the _kitchen_ .
5. Mein Vater ist im Badezimmer. My father is in the _bathroom_ .
6. Mein Bruder ist im Wohnzimmer. My brother is in the _living room_ .
7. Mein Hund Sherlock ist im Schlafzimmer. My dog Sherlock is in the _bedroom_ .

16 Look at the picture and write the words. Schau dir das Bild an und schreibe die Wörter auf.

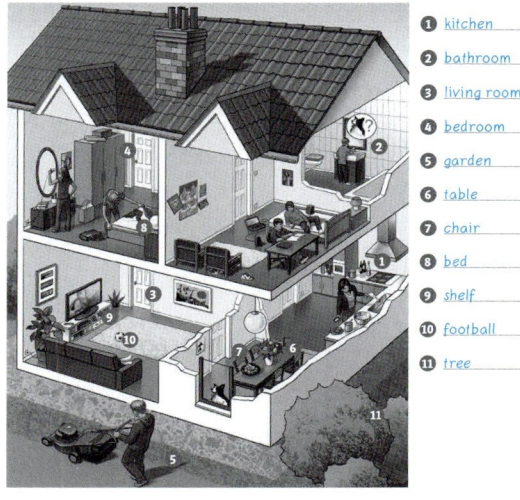

1. _kitchen_
2. _bathroom_
3. _living room_
4. _bedroom_
5. _garden_
6. _table_
7. _chair_
8. _bed_
9. _shelf_
10. _football_
11. _tree_

What's the word?

1. Ich bin im Esszimmer. I'm in the _dining room_ .
2. Lasst uns Tennis spielen. _Let's play_ tennis.
3. Ich mag das Spiel. I like the _game_ .
4. Es ist großartig. It's _great_ .
5. Schau mal! Da ist mein Hund. _Look_ ! There's my dog.
6. Er ist ein witziger Hund. He's a _funny_ dog.

17 Write the words. Finde die Wörter und schreibe sie auf Englisch und Deutsch auf.

1. ufynn _funny – lustig; witzig; merkwürdig; komisch_
2. kool _look – Schau mal_
3. htkans _thanks – danke_
4. mdrae _dream – Traum_
5. mega _game – Spiel_
6. nidign orom _dining room – Esszimmer_
7. etl's apyl _let's play – Lass(t) uns spielen_
8. egatr _great – großartig; toll_

18 Put in the right words. Setze die richtigen Wörter ein.

dining room	game	Let's play	Look	funny

1. Let's play a computer _game_ .
2. Ben the bat is _funny_ .
3. The table is in the _dining room_ .
4. _Look_ , this is our house.
5. _Let's play_ football in the garden.

What's the word?

1. Ich mag meine Eltern. I like my _parents_ .
2. Mein Onkel und meine Tante sind lustig. My _uncle_ and my _aunt_ are funny.
3. Ich habe einen Cousin. I have a _cousin_ .
4. Meine Großmutter ist cool. My _grandmother_ is cool.
5. Mein Großvater kommt aus Greenwich. My _grandfather_ is from Greenwich.

19 Right or wrong?

a) Look at page 194. Are the sentences right or wrong? Tick ✓ the right box.
Schaue dir Seite 194 im Buch an. Sind die Sätze richtig oder falsch? Kreuze ✓ an.

	right	wrong
1. Henry is Adam's grandfather.	✓	
2. Lisa is Adam's mum.	✓	
3. Sarah is Adam's brother.		✓
4. Isabel is Adam's sister.		✓
5. Matthew and Lucy are Helen and Kevin's parents.	✓	
6. Henry and Anne are Adam's grandparents.	✓	
7. Anne is Lucy's grandmother.		✓

b) Complete the sentences. Vervollständige die Sätze.

1. _Helen_ and _Kevin_ are Adam's cousins.
2. _Lucy_ is Adam's aunt.
3. _Lisa_ and _David_ are Adam's parents.
4. Daniel is Adam's _brother_ .
5. Isabel is an only child. She has no _brothers and sisters_ .
6. Lucy is Adam's _aunt_ and Matthew is Adam's _uncle_ .

20 Complete the words. Vervollständige die Wörter mit den fehlenden Buchstaben.

A	A	A	A	A	E	E	E	E	I	O	O	U	U	U

1. p a r e n t s   3. g r a n d m o t h e r   5. a u n t
2. u n c l e   4. c o u s i n   6. g r a n d f a t h e r

What's the word?

1. Der <u>Turnschuh</u> ist im <u>Kleiderschrank</u>. — The <u>trainer</u> is in the <u>wardrobe</u> .
2. Dein <u>Schal</u> auch. — Your <u>scarf</u> too.
3. Ich mag deinen <u>Teppich</u>. — I like your <u>carpet</u> .
4. — <u>lamp</u>
5. Da ist ein Geräusch. Es ist der <u>Wecker</u>. — There's a noise. It's the <u>alarm clock</u> .
6. — <u>hair straightener</u>
7. Das <u>Baumhaus</u> ist <u>fertig</u>. — The <u>tree house</u> is <u>ready</u> .
8. — <u>wood</u>

21 Complete the crossword. Vervollständige das Kreuzworträtsel.

Across ▶ :
3. English word for 'fertig'
5. English word for 'Lampe'
8.
10. ... is from trees.
11. One scarf, two ...

Down ▼ :
2.
6. Your mother and your father = your ...
7. A house in a tree is a ... .
9.
12. There's a in the tree house. Is it a bat?

Crossword answers:
1. CARPET
3. READY
5. LAMP
8. WARDROBE
10. WOOD
11. SCARVES
(Down) TREEHOUSE, TRAINER, ALARMCLOCK, PARENTS, LAMP, INCENSE...

What's the word?

1. Meine <u>Schule</u> ist toll. — My <u>school</u> is great.
2. Ich gehe auf die Thomas Tallis Schule. — I <u>go to</u> Thomas Tallis School.
3. Ich mag diesen <u>Ort</u>. — I like this <u>place</u> .
4. Ich bin in der 5. <u>Klasse</u>. — I'm in <u>Year</u> 7.
5. In Deutschland haben wir keine <u>Uniformen in der Schule</u>. — In Germany we have no <u>uniforms at school</u> .
6. Ich mag unsere <u>Cafeteria</u> in der Schule. — I like our <u>cafeteria</u> at school.
7. Hunde sind meine <u>Lieblingstiere</u>. — Dogs are my <u>favourite</u> animals.

1 About me. Stelle dich auf Englisch vor.

1. Hallo, ich heiße ... . <u>Hello. My name is (individuelle Lösung).</u>
2. Ich bin ... Jahre alt. <u>I'm (individuelle Lösung) years old.</u>
3. Ich komme aus ... . <u>I'm from (individuelle Lösung).</u>
4. Ich gehe auf die ... Schule. <u>I go to (individuelle Lösung).</u>
5. Ich bin in der fünften Klasse. <u>I'm in Year seven.</u>
6. Mein Lieblingstier ist ... . <u>My favourite animal is (individuelle Lösung).</u>

2 Look at the pictures and write the words. Schau dir die Bilder an und schreibe die Wörter auf.

This is my new <u>school</u> . | This is me in my <u>uniform</u> . | This is the <u>cafeteria</u> .
I <u>go</u> to a cool school. | It's OK. Blue is my <u>favourite</u> | It's my favourite <u>place</u>
I'm in <u>Year</u> 7. | colour. | at Thomas Tallis.

What's the word?

1. Wir haben einen tollen <u>Pausenhof</u> an unserer Schule. — We have a great <u>playground</u> at our school.
2. Ich kann in der Cafeteria <u>essen</u>. — I can <u>eat</u> in the cafeteria.
3. Ich mag das <u>Essen</u> dort. — I like the <u>food</u> there.
4. Mein <u>Klassenzimmer</u> ist neben dem Park. — My <u>classroom</u> is next to the park.
5. Herr <u>Swindon</u> ist unser <u>Klassenlehrer</u>. — <u>Mr</u> Swindon is our <u>tutor</u> .
6. Er ist <u>sehr</u> nett. — He's <u>very</u> nice.
7. Unser <u>Englischlehrer</u> ist auch nett. — Our <u>English teacher</u> is nice too.
8. Ich mag <u>Mathe</u>. — I like <u>Maths</u> .

3 Complete the words. Vervollständige die Wörter mit den fehlenden Buchstaben.

1. Mr Smith is our English t<u>e</u>a<u>c</u>h<u>er</u>. [A A A A A A]
2. My cl<u>a</u>ssr<u>oo</u>m is my f<u>a</u>v<u>ou</u>r<u>i</u>te pl<u>a</u>c<u>e</u>. [A A A E E E]
3. I like our t<u>u</u>t<u>o</u>r. [E E E E I I]
4. We play football in the pl<u>a</u>ygr<u>o</u>u<u>n</u>d. [O O O O O O]
5. We <u>e</u>a<u>t</u> in the c<u>a</u>f<u>e</u>t<u>e</u>r<u>i</u>a. [O U U U]
6. I like my new friends <u>a</u>t sch<u>oo</u>l.

4 Right or wrong? Richtig oder falsch?

Look at pages 32/33. Are the sentences right or wrong? Tick ✔ the right box. Correct the wrong words. Schau die die Seiten 32/33 im Buch an. Sind die Sätze richtig oder falsch? Kreuze ✔ an. Korrigiere die Wörter, die falsch sind.

	right	wrong	correction
1. The name of Holly's school is Thomas Tailor School.		✔	Tallis
2. Holly's school uniform is black and green.		✔	blue
3. Mr Swindon is her English teacher and her tutor.		✔	Maths
4. Holly's favourite place is the playground.	✔		
5. She's in tutor group 7RS.	✔		

What's the word?

1. Ich <u>spreche</u> gern mit meinem Freund Luke. — I like to <u>talk to</u> my friend Luke.
2. Frau Warren ist die <u>Hausmeisterin</u> an unserer Schule. — <u>Mrs</u> Warren is the <u>caretaker</u> at our school.
3. Ich <u>singe</u> gerne. — I like to <u>sing</u> .
4. Ich gehe mit meinen Freunden ins <u>Tonstudio</u>. — I go to the <u>recording studio</u> with my friends.
5. Ich mag Fußball <u>nicht</u>. — <u>I don't like</u> football.
6. Es sind 28 <u>Schüler</u> in unserer <u>Klasse</u>. — There are 28 <u>students</u> in our <u>tutor group</u> .

5 Look at the pictures and write the verbs. Schau dir die Bilder an und schreibe die Verben auf.

<u>go</u> | <u>talk</u> | <u>sing</u> | <u>eat</u>

6 Find the words. Knacke den Code und finde die Wörter. Zu jeder Zahl gehört ein Buchstabe.

1. <u>S I N G</u>
   11 5 8 6
2. <u>T U T O R   G R O U P</u>
   13 15 13 4 9   6 9 4 15 12
3. <u>S T U D E N T</u>
   11 13 15 3 2 8 13
4. <u>C A R E T A K E R</u>
   14 7 9 2 13 7 10 2 9
5. <u>R E C O R D I N G   S T U D I O</u>
   9 2 14 4 9 3 5 8 6   11 13 15 3 5 4
6. <u>T A L K</u>
   13 7 1 10

A	C	D	E	G	I	K	L
7	14	3	2	6	5	10	1

N	O	P	R	S	T	U
8	4	12	9	11	13	15

What's the word?

1. Ich kaufe ein Lineal für Mathe. — I buy a *ruler* for Maths.
2. Ich kaufe einen Füller, einen Buntstift und einen Radiergummi für die Schule. — I buy a *pen*, a *pencil* and an *eraser* for school.
3. Ich mag meine Tasche. — I like my *bag*.
4. Für Englisch haben wir zwei Übungshefte. — We have two *exercise books* for English.

7 Look at the pictures and write the words in English and German. Schau dir die Bilder an und schreibe die Wörter auf Englisch und Deutsch.

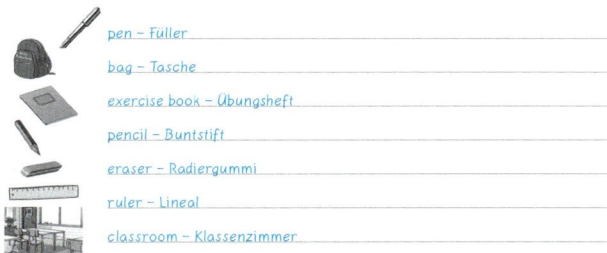

pen – Füller

bag – Tasche

exercise book – Übungsheft

pencil – Buntstift

eraser – Radiergummi

ruler – Lineal

classroom – Klassenzimmer

8 Put in the right words. Setze die richtigen Wörter ein.

exercise books	cafeteria	school	students	pencils
classrooms	food	favourite	Maths	ruler
teacher	recording studio	bag		

At _school_

There are 430 _students_ and 20 _classrooms_ in our school.

We have a _cafeteria_ and a _recording studio_. The _food_ is great.

My _favourite_ teacher is Mr Swandon. He is my Maths _teacher_.

For _Maths_ we buy a _ruler_ and _pencils_. All my things are in my

new _bag_ – the _exercise books_ too.

What's the word?

1. Ich sitze neben dem Fenster. — I _sit_ next to the _window_.
2. Sprich bitte nicht mit ihr. — _Don't talk_ to her, please.
3. Bitte singe nicht. — Don't sing, _please_.
4. Mein Name ist David. Nenn mich Dave. — My name is David. _Call me_ Dave.
5. Dave ist ein guter Sänger. — Dave is a _good singer_.
6. Er kann auch tanzen. — He can _dance_ too.
7. Macht bitte eure Übungshefte zu. — _Close_ your exercise books, please.

9 Look at the pictures and complete the sentences. Schau dir die Bilder an und vervollständige die Sätze.

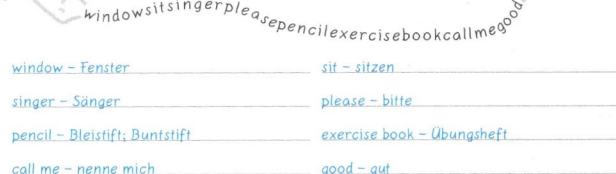

1. Don't _talk_ to your friends, please.
2. Don't _open_ the window, please.
3. Don't _sit_ on the chair, please.
4. Don't _eat_ in the classroom, please.
5. Don't _sing / dance_ now, please.

10 Find the words. Write the English and German words. Finde die Wörter. Schreibe sie auf Englisch und Deutsch auf.

windowsitsingerpleasepencilexercisebookcallmegood

window – Fenster	_sit – sitzen_
singer – Sänger	_please – bitte_
pencil – Bleistift; Buntstift	_exercise book – Übungsheft_
call me – nenne mich	_good – gut_

What's the word?

1. Ich mag Fußball wirklich. — I _really_ like football.
2. Es ist für dich. — It's _for_ you.
3. boy ⟷ — _girl_
4. Rede jetzt bitte nicht. — Don't talk _now_, please.
5. Setz dich neben mich. — _Sit down_ next to me.
6. Schau dir Luke an. Er hat ein grünes Fahrrad. — _Look at_ Luke. He has a green bike.
7. Der Talentwettbewerb ist nächste Woche. — The _talent show_ is _next week_.
8. Schlagt bitte eure Bücher auf. — _Open_ your books, please.
9. Und nehmt eure Übungshefte heraus. — And _take out_ your exercise books.

11 My Wednesday at school.
Put in the verbs and put the sentences in the correct order.
Setze die Verben ein und bringe die Sätze in die richtige Reihenfolge.

sit down	go	play	talk	open	take out	look at

I _go_ to school. ☐ 1

I don't _talk_ and I _look at_ my teacher Mr Swindon. ☐ 4

I _sit down_ next to my friend and I _open_ my bag. ☐ 2

I go home and _play_ football in the garden. ☐ 5

I _take out_ my exercise book and my pen. Mr Swindon is here now. ☐ 3

12 Write the words. Finde die Wörter und schreibe sie auf Englisch und Deutsch auf.

1. aket uot _take out – herausnehmen_
2. latent wsoh _talent show – Talentwettbewerb_
3. sti wond _sit down – sich hinsetzen_
4. lleyra _really – wirklich_
5. lgir _girl – Mädchen_

What's the word?

1. Schaut bitte an die Tafel. — Please look at the _board_.
2. Bitte meldet euch. — _Put your hands up_, please.
3. Ich kann Nummer 1, 2 und 5 machen. — I can _do_ number 1, 2 and 5.
4. Ich kann Aufgabe 1 in mein Übungsheft schreiben. — I can _write_ exercise 1 in my exercise book.
5. Es sind drei Schüler in der Gruppe. — There are three students in the _group_.
6. Es gibt eine Show in Greewich. — There is a _show_ in Greewich.
7. Wo ist mein Buch? – Bitte schön. — Where is my book? – _Here you are_.
8. Danke, Luke. — _Thank you_, Luke.
9. Kaufe ein Übungsheft! — Buy _an_ exercise book!

13 Match the sentence parts. Ordne die Satzteile zu.

1. Holly is in — e) my group.
2. Write — f) your name, please.
3. Look — a) at the board, please.
4. Who can do — c) number five?
5. Put — b) your hands up, please.
6. Thank — d) you, Mr Swindon.

14 Look at the pictures and write the words in English and German. Schau dir die Bilder an und schreibe die Wörter auf Englisch und Deutsch auf.

write – schreiben   _board – Tafel_   _show – Show_   _girl – Mädchen_

What's the word?

1. Ich habe zehn <u>Finger</u>. — I have ten <u>fingers</u>
2. Aber nur zwei <u>Hände</u>. — But only two <u>hands</u>.
3. Ich <u>höre</u> gerne Musik. — I like to <u>listen to</u> music.
4. Aber ich habe kein Lieblings<u>lied</u>. — But I don't have a favourite <u>song</u>.
5. <u>Lies</u> bitte die <u>Frage</u>. — <u>Read</u> the <u>question</u>, please.
6. Dann <u>sag</u> bitte die <u>Antwort</u>. — Then <u>say</u> the <u>answer</u>, please.
7. <u>Legt</u> bitte die Stifte auf den Tisch. — <u>Put</u> the pens on the table, please.

15 Find ten words.

a) Find the English words. (↓ and →) Finde die englischen Wörter.

S	G	A	F	F	H	A	N	D	S
F	W	N	Y	I	Y	F	Q	H	A
S	R	S	H	N	D	L	U	I	Y
O	I	W	F	G	F	R	E	A	D
N	T	E	L	E	L	Z	S	H	A
G	E	R	X	R	P	U	T	F	I
F	T	Z	P	S	L	G	I	P	L
L	I	S	T	E	N	R	O	O	O
Z	F	C	R	D	W	S	N	U	P

b) Write the words. Schreibe die Wörter auf.

<u>fingers, hand(s), say, answer, question, read, put, song, listen, write</u>

16 Look at the pictures and write the words in English and German. Schau dir die Bilder an und schreibe die Wörter auf Englisch und Deutsch auf.

<u>hand – Hand</u> <u>finger – Finger</u> <u>question – Frage</u> <u>answer – Antwort</u>

What's the word?

1. Schau, das ist mein <u>Stundenplan</u>. — Look, this is my <u>timetable</u>
2. — <u>day</u>
3. Am <u>Montag</u> haben wir <u>Englisch</u>. — On <u>Monday</u> we have <u>English</u>
4. Mein Lieblings<u>fach</u> ist Musik. — My favourite <u>subject</u> is <u>Music</u>.
5. Am <u>Dienstag</u> haben wir <u>Sportunterricht</u>. — On <u>Tuesday</u> we have <u>PE</u>
6. Wir haben <u>Herrn Swindon</u> in <u>Mathe</u>. — We have Mr Swindon for <u>Maths</u>
7. <u>Frau Maier</u> ist unsere <u>Deutschlehrerin</u>. — Mrs Maier is our <u>German</u> teacher.
8. Am <u>Mittwoch</u> haben wir <u>Französisch</u>. — On <u>Wednesday</u> we have <u>French</u>.
9. Am <u>Donnerstag</u> haben wir <u>Technik</u>. — On <u>Thursday</u> we have <u>Design Technology</u>.
10. Am <u>Freitag</u> haben wir <u>Naturwissenschaft</u> und <u>Kunst</u>. — On <u>Friday</u> we have <u>Science</u> and <u>Art</u>.
11. Am <u>Samstag</u> und <u>Sonntag</u> haben wir keine Schule. — On <u>Saturday</u> and <u>Sunday</u> we have no school.

17 Write the days of the week.

a) Write the days. Schreibe die Tage auf.

1. <u>Wednes</u>day 3. <u>Satur</u>day 5. <u>Fri</u>day 7. <u>Tues</u>day
2. <u>Mon</u>day 4. <u>Sun</u>day 6. <u>Thurs</u>day

b) Write the days in the right order. Schreibe die Tage in der richtigen Reihenfolge auf.

<u>Monday, Tuesday, Wednesday, Thursday, Friday, Saturday, Sunday</u>

18 Put a circle around the odd one out. Welches Wort passt nicht in die Reihe? Kreise es ein.

1. Monday · Friday · Tuesday · (days) · Saturday
2. Art · Music · Design Technology · Science · (classroom)
3. classroom · cafeteria · playground · (board)
4. French · English · (Maths) · German

What's the word?

1. In der Pause gehe ich auf den Pausenhof. — <u>At break</u> I go to the playground.
2. Sportunterricht ist meine nächste Schulstunde. Und deine? — PE is my next <u>lesson</u>. And <u>yours</u>?
3. Französisch ist einfach. — French is <u>easy</u>.
4. Es ist wie Deutsch. — It's <u>like</u> German.
5. Du hast Recht. — You're <u>right</u>.
6. Ich bin auch gut in Französisch. — <u>I am good at</u> French too.
7. Das ist kein Witz. — That's <u>not</u> a <u>joke</u>.
8. Kannst du Rechtschreibung buchstabieren? — Can you <u>spell spelling</u>?
9. Nein, aber ich kann 'Alphabet' buchstabieren. — No, but I can spell <u>alphabet</u>.
10. Ich mag Kunst; es ist interessant. — I like Art; it's <u>interesting</u>.
11. Am Dienstag haben wir Kunst. — <u>On Tuesday</u> we have Art.
12. Frau Kapoor macht die Überprüfung der Anwesenheit. — <u>Registration</u> is with <u>Ms</u> Kapoor.

19 Complete the words. Vervollständige die Wörter mit den fehlenden Buchstaben.

A A A A A E E E E E E E E E E E I I
I I I I O
O U

1. sp<u>e</u>ll<u>i</u>ng
2. r<u>e</u>g<u>i</u>str<u>a</u>t<u>i</u>on
3. l<u>e</u>ss<u>o</u>n
4. <u>a</u>lph<u>a</u>b<u>e</u>t
5. <u>i</u>nt<u>e</u>r<u>e</u>st<u>i</u>ng
6. t<u>i</u>m<u>e</u>t<u>a</u>bl<u>e</u>
7. s<u>u</u>bj<u>e</u>ct
8. j<u>o</u>k<u>e</u>

20 Choose the right answer. Kreuze die für dich zutreffenden Aussagen an.

1. I'm good at … English ☐ Music ☐ Maths ☐ Art ☐ <u>(individuelle Lösung)</u> ☐
2. Science ☐ Design Technology ☐ <u>(individuelle Lösung)</u> ☐ … is/are interesting.
3. I don't like <u>(individuelle Lösung)</u>.
4. My timetable is … great ☐ good ☐ not good ☐.

What's the word?

1. Das <u>Mittagessen</u> zu Hause ist gut. — <u>Lunch</u> at home is good.
2. Mein <u>Onkel</u> ist aus England. — My <u>uncle</u> is from England.
3. Ich <u>sehe</u> ihn zu Hause. — I <u>see</u> him at home.
4. Lass uns einen <u>Streich</u> spielen. — Let's play a <u>trick</u>.
5. Wir <u>alle</u> mögen <u>Filme</u> und Musik. — We <u>all</u> like <u>films</u> and music.
6. — <u>saxophone</u>
7. — <u>winner</u>
8. Ich kann <u>Freundschaften</u> mit den Schülern aus meiner Klasse <u>schließen</u>. — I can <u>make friends with</u> the students in my tutor group.
9. Ich mag <u>Kaugummi</u>. — I like <u>chewing gum</u>.
10. — <u>jeans</u>

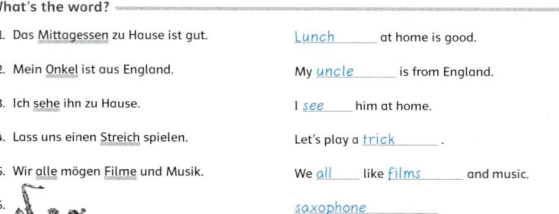

21 Match the words. Ordne die Wörter richtig zu.

1. see — a) Monday
2. week — b) talk
3. uncle — c) look
4. say — d) family
5. trick — e) food
6. saxophone — f) T-shirt
7. jeans — g) fun/funny
8. lunch — h) music

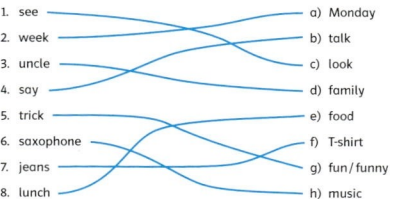

22 Put a circle around the odd one out. Welches Wort passt nicht in die Reihe? Kreise es ein.

1. one · three · (all) · seven
2. bat · cat · guinea pig · (girl)
3. (jeans) · ruler · pen · eraser
4. Maths · English · (lunch) · Science
5. playground · classroom · cafeteria · (bedroom)
6. sing · talk · say · (see)
7. Monday · (film) · Tuesday · Friday
8. (chewing gum) · good · interesting · funny
9. caretaker · (uncle) · student · teacher
10. lesson · subject · (dog) · timetable

What's the word?

1. Ich kaufe einen <u>Taschenrechner</u> für Mathe. I buy a <u>calculator</u> for Maths.
2. In meinem <u>Federmäppchen</u> ist ein <u>Filzstift</u> und ein <u>Anspitzer</u>. In my <u>pencil case</u> there is a <u>felt-tip</u> and a <u>pencil sharpener</u>.
3. Ich kaufe <u>Klebstoff</u> für den <u>Religionsunterricht</u>. I buy <u>glue</u> for <u>RE</u>.
4. Mein <u>Lieblingsfach</u> ist <u>Informationstechnik</u>. My favourite subject is <u>IT</u>.
5. <u>Geschichte</u> und <u>Biologie</u> mag ich auch. I like <u>History</u> and <u>Biology</u> too.
6. <u>Erdkunde</u> ist <u>langweilig</u>. <u>Geography</u> is <u>boring</u>.
7. <u>Französisch</u> ist <u>schwierig</u>. French is <u>difficult</u>.

23 Complete the crossword. Vervollständige das Kreuzworträtsel.

Across ▶ :
5. [image]
8. Short form: Information Technology
10. English word for 'Biologie'

Down ▼ :
1.
3. Short form: Religious Education
4. [image]
7. English word for 'Geschichte'
2. [image]
6. [image]
9. interesting ⟷

Crossword solution:
- 5 ▶ P E N C I L S H A R P E N E R
- Down 1: P N C I L C A S E
- 6: G A L C U L A T O R
- 7: H U E S T O R Y
- 3: R I S T
- 4: F E L T - T I P
- 10 ▶ B I O L O G Y
- 8 ▶ I T
- 9: B O R I N G

What's the word?

1. Wir haben <u>Spaß</u>. We have <u>fun</u>.
2. Was ist <u>ein Talent</u>? What's your <u>talent</u>?
3. <u>Gut gemacht!</u> <u>Well done</u> !
4. Michael Jackson ist ein <u>Star</u>. Michael Jackson is a <u>star</u>.
5. Ich mag <u>indisches</u> Essen. I like <u>Indian</u> food.
6. Lass uns in ein <u>Restaurant</u> gehen. Let's go to a <u>restaurant</u>.

24 Find ten words.

a) Find the English words. (↓ and →) Finde die englischen Wörter.

F	H	T	R	I	C	K	F	W	I	S
T	W	P	S	A	W	J	I	K	A	A
R	E	S	T	A	U	R	A	N	T	X
Y	L	G	A	B	T	F	Y	N	K	O
L	L	H	R	N	A	U	L	E	L	P
F	D	S	H	F	L	N	F	R	U	H
D	O	F	X	M	E	N	X	G	N	O
I	N	D	I	A	N	S	I	H	C	N
W	E	L	I	H	T	X	D	J	H	E

b) Write the words in English and German. Schreibe die Wörter auf Englisch und Deutsch auf.

<u>trick – Streich; Trick</u> <u>restaurant – Restaurant</u>
<u>winner – Gewinner(in); Sieger(in)</u> <u>talent – Talent</u>
<u>saxophone – Saxophon</u> <u>Indian – indisch</u>
<u>Well done! – Gut gemacht!</u> <u>fun – Spaß</u>
<u>star – Star</u> <u>lunch – Mittagessen</u>

What's the word?

1. Nach dem <u>Mittagessen</u> spiele ich <u>Korbball</u>. <u>After</u> lunch I play <u>netball</u>.
2. Meine <u>Mannschaft</u> ist toll. My <u>team</u> is great.
3. Ich <u>liebe</u> Korbball. Es ist toll zu <u>gewinnen</u>. I <u>love</u> netball. It's great to <u>win</u>.
4. Wir gewinnen <u>viel</u>. We win <u>a lot</u>.
5. In meiner <u>Freizeit</u> mache ich Musik. In my <u>free time</u> I play music.
6. <u>Mittwochs</u> habe ich <u>Musikprobe</u>. <u>On Wednesdays</u> I have music <u>practice</u>.
7. Ich <u>will</u> eine gute Sängerin sein. I <u>want to</u> be a good singer.
8. Elton John ist sehr <u>berühmt</u>. Elton John is very <u>famous</u>.

1 Put in the right words. Setze die richtigen Wörter ein.

| play | after | Friday | Thursday | see you | netball practice | on Wednesdays |

Luke: Let's <u>play</u> football on Wednesday.
Dave: No. <u>On Wednesdays</u> I have <u>netball practice</u>. Are you at home on Thursday?
Luke: No, sorry. On <u>Thursday</u> I play tennis with Holly. Friday?
Dave: OK, <u>Friday</u> is good. Let's play <u>after</u> lunch.
Luke: OK, <u>see you</u>.

2 Find the words. Write the English and German words.
Finde die Wörter. Schreibe sie auf Englisch und Deutsch auf.

famouswantteamnetballafterfreetimepracticelove

<u>famous – berühmt</u> <u>after – nach</u>
<u>want – wollen</u> <u>free time – Freizeit</u>
<u>team – Mannschaft; Team</u> <u>practice – Übung; Training</u>
<u>netball – Korbball</u> <u>love – lieben; gern mögen</u>

What's the word?

1. Ich gehe in der <u>Mittagspause</u> nach Hause. I go home at <u>lunchtime</u>.
2. Nach dem Mittagessen <u>renne</u> ich mit meinem Hund. After lunch I <u>run</u> with my dog.
3. Ich <u>renne</u> viel <u>herum</u>. I <u>run around</u> a lot.
4. Ich bin der <u>Kapitän</u> meines Korbballteams. I'm the <u>captain</u> of my netball team.
5. <u>Mittwochs</u> gehen wir in unserer Freizeit ins <u>Tierheim</u>. On Wednesdays we go to <u>animal rescue shelter</u> in our free time.
6. Wir lieben es, den Tieren dort zu <u>helfen</u>. We love to <u>help</u> the animals there.
7. Wir <u>helfen jede</u> Woche. We help <u>every</u> week.

3 Match the sentence parts. Ordne die Satzteile zu.

1. I sing and dance — a) Luke on Fridays.
2. I play football with — b) mother on Saturdays.
3. I run with my dog — c) practice on Tuesdays.
4. I sing songs in the recording — d) on Sundays.
5. I buy new jeans with my — e) Sherlock every day.
6. I go to netball — f) cafeteria on Thursdays.
7. I eat at the — g) tutor on Mondays.
8. I talk to my — h) studio on Wednesdays.

4 Complete the words. Vervollständige die Wörter mit den fehlenden Buchstaben und übersetze sie ins Deutsche.

| A | A | A | A | E | E | E | E | E | E | E | E | I | I | I |

| O | U | U | U | U | Y |

1. <u>e</u>v<u>e</u>r<u>y</u> jede(r)
2. c<u>a</u>pt<u>a</u>in Kapitän
3. r<u>u</u>n <u>a</u>r<u>o</u>und herumrennen
4. l<u>u</u>ncht<u>i</u>m<u>e</u> Mittagspause
5. h<u>e</u>lp helfen
6. fr<u>e</u><u>e</u>t<u>i</u>m<u>e</u> Freizeit
7. t<u>e</u><u>a</u>m Team; Mannschaft
8. r<u>u</u>n rennen

yummy !

What's the word?

1. Wir haben eine Cafeteria in der Schule. — We have a cafeteria _at_ school.
2. Am Wochenende haben wir keine Schule. Das ist toll. — _At the weekend_ we don't have school. That's great.
3. Ich gehe mit meinen Freunden jeden Monat ins Kino. — I go to the _cinema_ with my friends every _month_.
4. Dort sehen wir uns Filme an. — We _watch movies_ there.
5. Zu Hause sehe ich viel fern. — I _watch TV_ a lot at home.
6. Ich mag die Sendungen mit Sängern. — I like the _programmes_ with singers.
7. Ich mag auch Science-Fiction. — I like _science fiction_ too.

5 Cross the odd one out. Ein Wort ist falsch. Streiche es durch.

1. I like TV. / ~~month.~~ / science fiction.
2. I see my friends at ~~science fiction~~ / school. / the weekend.
3. We watch movies. / TV. / ~~songs.~~
4. It's time for my favourite programme. / ~~recording studio.~~ / show.

6 Make sentences. Bilde Sätze über deine Aktivitäten.

| I watch |
| I buy |
| I play |
| I sing |
| I eat |
| I go |
| I read |

| every day. |
| at the weekend. |
| on Mondays. |
| on … |

(individuelle Lösung)

What's the word?

1. Wir gehen gerne in den Zoo. — We like to go to the _zoo_.
2. Die Elefanten sind toll. — The _elephants_ are great.
3. Sie kommen aus Indien. — They _come_ from _India_.
4. Sie haben auch Pferde aus Deutschland. — They have _horses_ from Germany too.
5. Die Affen sind lustig. — The _monkeys_ are funny.
6. Die Tiger sind neben den Affen. — The _tigers_ are next to the monkeys.
7. Sie haben fünf Bären im Zoo. — They have five _bears_ at the zoo.
8. Schau, und da ist eine grüne Schlange. — Look, and there's a green _snake_.

7 Write the words. Finde die Wörter und schreibe sie auf Englisch und Deutsch auf.

1. myneok _monkey – Affe_
2. ozo _zoo – Zoo_
3. eaehtlnp _elephant – Elefant_
4. ndlia _India – Indien_
5. osehr _horse – Pferd_
6. gteri _tiger – Tiger_
7. seakn _snake – Schlange_
8. erab _bear – Bär_

8 Make sentences about animals you like. Schreibe auf, welche Tiere du magst und welche nicht.
Beginne mit

I like/I don't like …

(individuelle Lösung)

What's the word?

1. Es gibt noch mehr Tiere im Zoo. Die Papageien sind rot, grün, gelb und blau. — There are more animals in the zoo. The _parrots_ are red, green, yellow and blue.
2. Sie sind elf Jahre alt. — They are eleven _years old_.
3. Papageien sind Vögel. — _Parrots_ are _birds_.
4. Die Giraffen sind sehr groß. — The _giraffes_ are very _high_.
5. Sie sind fünf Meter groß. — They are five _metres high_.
6. Die Pinguine sind schwarz und weiß. — The _penguins_ are black and white.
7. Schlangen essen Mäuse. — _Snakes_ eat _mice_.
8. Schau, da ist ein Bär mit einem Fisch. — Look, there's a bear with a _fish_.
9. Meine Maus ist zwei Jahre alt. — My _mouse_ is two years old.

9 Put the animals in the right box. Ordne die Tiere dem richtigen Kasten zu.
Einige Tiere können auch auf beiden Seiten stehen.

| bat | cat | dog | fish | elephant | penguin | horse | tiger |
| bear | bird | giraffe | monkey | snake | parrot | mouse |

Zoo	Germany
elephant	bat
penguin	cat
tiger	dog
bear	fish
giraffe	horse
monkey	snake
snake	mouse
parrot; bird	bird

10 Write the words. Schreibe die Mehrzahl auf.

one tiger – two _tigers_   one mouse – two _mice_
one monkey – three _monkeys_   one fish – five _fish_

What's the word?

1. Ich bin zwölf Jahre alt. — I'm _twelve_ years old.
2. Mein Vater ist fünfundvierzig Jahre alt. — My father is _forty-five_ years old.
3. Meine Großmutter ist achtundsiebzig Jahre alt. — My grandmother is _seventy-eight_ years old.
4. Mein Onkel ist dreiundfünfzig Jahre alt. — My uncle is _fifty-three_ years old.
5. Meine Schwester ist siebzehn Jahre alt. — My sister is _seventeen_ years old.
6. Unser Haus ist die Nummer neunundneunzig. — Our house is number _ninety-nine_.
7. Es gibt fünfzehn Spieler in unserer Korbballmannschaft. — There are _fifteen_ players in our netball team.
8. Es gibt einhundert Lehrer an unserer Schule. — There are _one hundred_ teachers at our school.

11 Circle the numbers and write the words.

a) Find the numbers and put a circle around them. Finde die Zahlen und kreise sie ein.

12	13	93	99	16	76	(10)	37	(95)
(88)	64	99	45	(83)	17	25	64	21
59	22	45	12	76	51	21	(69)	59
(11)	12	85	(32)	81	(55)	22	14	33
37	77	39	51	(34)	66	22	21	85
43	37	38	21	33	45	71	62	51
21	(20)	33	(67)	81	(18)	33	35	71
85	14	77	12	13	(15)	22	22	33
25	43	(46)	16	14	(31)	59	99	38

1. eighteen
2. thirty-two
3. ninety-five
4. forty-six
5. twenty
6. thirty-four
7. eighty-three
8. eleven
9. ten
10. fifteen
11. fifty-five
12. sixty-nine
13. thirty-one
14. eighty-eight
15. sixty-seven

b) Write the blue numbers in words. Schreibe die blauen Zahlen als Wörter auf.

ninety-three   _thirty-nine_

thirty-five   _twenty-five_

What's the word?

1. Lass uns über Essen sprechen. Ich liebe Obst. Und du? — Let's talk about food. I love fruit. And you?
2. Tiger essen gern Fleisch. — Tigers like to eat meat.
3. Ein Tiger isst 7 Kilogramm täglich. — A tiger eats 7 kilograms a day.
4. Pferde essen Gras. — Horses eat grass.
5. Elefanten essen auch Gras. — Elephants also eat grass.
6. Affen lieben Bananen. — Monkeys love bananas.
7.  — plant
8. — water

12 What do the animals eat? Write the words. Schreibe auf, was die Tiere essen.

fish   meat   plants, grass, fruit   grass

bananas   meat   mice, meat

13 Complete the words. Vervollständige die Wörter mit den fehlenden Buchstaben und übersetze sie ins Deutsche.

1. meat — Fleisch   A A A
2. plant — Pflanze   A A A
3. also — auch
4. banana — Banane   A E E
5. fruit — Obst   I O U
6. water — Wasser

What's the word?

1. Ich schlafe gerne. — I like to sleep.
2. Am Wochenende schlafe ich lang. — At the weekend I sleep long.
3. Edgar schläft vier Stunden täglich. — Edgar sleeps four hours a day.
4. Das ist nicht viel. — That isn't much.
5. Ich habe nur eine Schwester. — I only have one sister.
6. Meine Mutter redet nicht über ihr Alter. — My mother doesn't talk about her age.
7. Informationen über Blacky, das Pferd: — Information about Blacky, the horse:
8. Es kann 40 Kilometer pro Stunde laufen. — It can run 40 kilometres an hour.
9. Es ist 110 Zentimeter lang. — It is 110 centimetres long.

14 Put in the right words. Setzte die richtigen Wörter ein.

hour   an   long   much   only   a

1. My ruler is thirty centimetres long.
2. They only like bananas.
3. He sleeps an hour a day.
4. We have lessons five days a week.
5. I don't eat much.
6. Can you run forty kilometres an hour?

15 Look at the pictures and write the words in English and German. Schau dir die Bilder an und schreibe die Wörter auf Englisch und Deutsch auf.

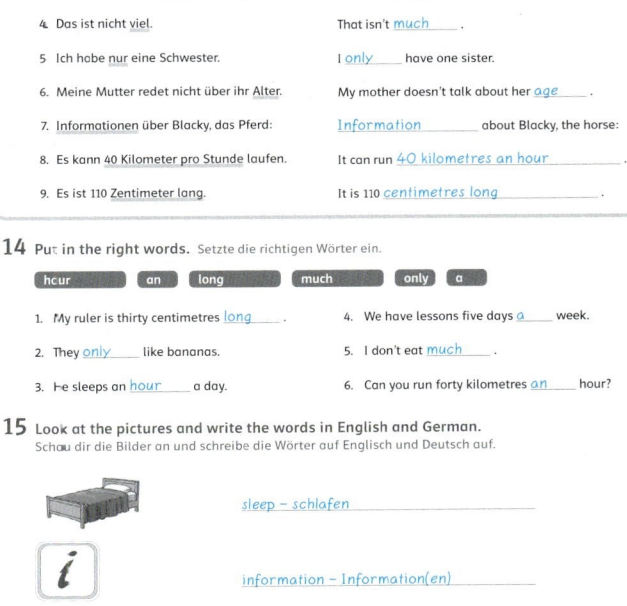

sleep – schlafen

information – Information(en)

fruit – Obst

centimetres – Zentimeter

What's the word?

1. Hier ist Lizzys Steckbrief. — Here's Lizzy's profile.
2. Sie lebt im Zoo. — She lives in the zoo.
3. Sie isst kleine Tiere. — She eats small animals.
4. Sie ist aus Afrika. — She's from Africa.
5. Im Winter schläft sie fünf Monate lang. — In winter she sleeps for five months.
6. Dann arbeiten die Tierpfleger nicht mit Lizzy. — Then the zookeepers don't work with Lizzy.
7. Lass uns über andere Tiere sprechen. — Let's talk about other animals.

16 Find seven words.

a) Find the English words. (↓ and →) Finde die englischen Wörter.

D	Z	A	D	C	E	I
S	O	S	N	A	P	B
W	O	R	K	F	R	S
P	K	E	K	R	O	M
N	E	L	W	I	F	A
B	E	T	I	C	I	L
O	P	N	N	A	L	L
T	E	O	T	H	E	R
E	R	Q	E	L	O	P
N	W	I	R	X	U	C

b) Write the words in English and German. Schreibe die Wörter auf Deutsch und Englisch auf.

zookeeper – Tierpfleger; Tierpflegerin
other – andere; weitere
winter – Winter
Africa – Afrika
profile – Profil; Steckbrief
small – klein
work – arbeiten

What's the word?

1. Luke: Ich stehe um sieben Uhr auf. — Luke: I get up at seven o'clock.
2. Dave: Das ist früh. — Dave: That's early.
3. Luke: Wann stehst du auf? — Luke: When do you get up?
4. Dave: Um acht. Danach gehe ich in die Schule. — Dave: At eight. After that I go to school.
5. Luke: Ich frühstücke zuerst. — Luke: First I have breakfast.
6. Danach füttere ich meinen Hund. — After that I feed my dog.
7. Dave: Warum putzt du deine Schuhe? — Dave: Why do you clean your shoes?
8. Luke: Sie sind schmutzig. Es ist Zeit zu gehen. — Luke: They are dirty. It's time to go.
9. Dave: Lass uns jetzt zu Mittag essen. — Dave: Let's have lunch now.

17 Look at the pictures and write the words. Schau dir die Bilder an und schreibe die Wörter auf.

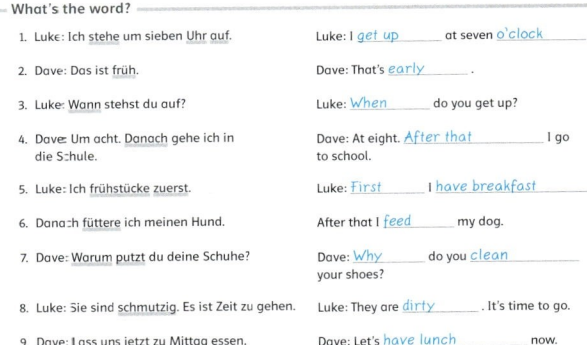

I get up at eight o'clock. First I eat a banana.
After that I go to the bathroom. Then I feed my cat. She sleeps in my bed. She loves to play with me. After breakfast I clean her toilet.
Then I go to school. I am at school at nine o'clock.

18 What time is it? Write sentences. Wie spät ist es? Schreibe Sätze.

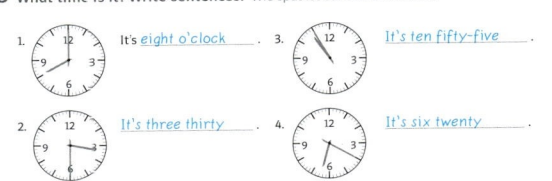

1. It's eight o'clock.
2. It's three thirty.
3. It's ten fifty-five.
4. It's six twenty.

What's the word?

1. Ich befrage meinen Mathelehrer. — I interview my Maths teacher.
2. Es ist ein ausgefüllter Tag. — It's a busy day.
3. Du kannst es in der Schulzeitschrift lesen. — You can read it in the school magazine.
4. Wir sprechen über Papas Arbeit. — We talk about dad's work.
5. Jeden Montagnachmittag ist er an der Schule. — Every Monday afternoon he's at school.
6. Die Lehrer haben ihr Zimmer neben der Cafeteria. — The teachers have their room next to the cafeteria.
7. — cage
8. Wie spät ist es? — What time is it?
9. Es ist fünf Uhr. Lass uns Tee trinken. — It's five o'clock. Let's have tea.

19 Find the words. Write the English and German words.
Finde die Wörter. Schreibe sie auf Englisch und Deutsch auf.

o'clockwhyfirst

profilecagebreakfastmagazineafternoonearlyworkcleaninterview

profile – Steckbrief	cage – Käfig
breakfast – Frühstück	magazine – Zeitschrift
afternoon – Nachmittag	early – früh
work – Arbeit	clean – sauber machen
interview – befragen	o'clock – Uhr
why – warum	first – zuerst

20 Make sentences. Schreibe auf, was du jeden Tag machst.

I clean the kitchen every day.

(individuelle Lösung)

What's the word?

1. Lasst uns am Samstag in das Café gehen. — Let's go to the café on Saturday.
2. Okay. Danach möchte ich den Hund ausführen. — OK. After that I want to take the dog for a walk.
3. Wie alt ist dein Hund? — How old is your dog?
4. Ich weiß es nicht. — I don't know.
5. Er mag Nüsse. — He likes nuts.
6. Und er ist der schnellste Hund im Park. — And he is the fastest dog in the park.
7. Ich mag die Geschichte nicht. — I don't like the story.
8. Der Polizeibeamte findet einen Hinweis. — The police officer finds a clue.
9. Da sind Waschbären in dem Loch. — There are raccoons in the hole.

21 Right or wrong?

a) Look at the pictures on page 63. Are the sentences right or wrong? Tick ✓ the right box.
Schau dir die Bilder auf Seite 63 im Buch an. Sind die Sätze richtig oder falsch? Kreuze ✓ an.

	right	wrong
1. There is a banana in the café.		✓
2. Mrs Abrihim talks to a police officer.	✓	
3. Sherlock looks at the police officer.	✓	
4. There is a hole in the ceiling.	✓	
5. Luke has a plant in his hands.		✓
6. There is a mess in the café.	✓	
7. There is only one box.		✓
8. A raccoon runs in the picture.	✓	
9. The chairs are blue.	✓	
10. The café's name is Aladin's Park Café.		✓

b) What's not in the story? Underline the words. Unterstreiche alle Wörter, die nicht in der Geschichte vorkommen oder auf keinem Bild auf Seite 63 zu sehen sind.

1. raccoon, birds, dog, snake, bear, fish
2. chair, tables, shelf, boxes, bed
3. boy, girl, man, woman, pet, police officer
4. park, school, café, zoo, playground

What's the word?

1. Lasst uns das Rätsel lösen. — Let's solve the mystery.
2. Wir können uns nach Spuren umsehen. — We can look around for clues.
3. Schaue zur Decke! — Look at the ceiling!
4. Du kannst mich anrufen. — You can call me.

22 Put in the right words.

a) Put in the right words in English and German. Setze die richtigen Wörter auf Englisch und Deutsch ein.

clue | ceiling | raccoon | hole | café | solve | nuts
mess | football | help | look around | police officer | park

1. The noise is a racoon – Waschbär.
2. Sherlock finds a clue – Hinweis.
3. There are nuts – Nüsse in the café.
4. Then they go to Mrs Abrihim's café – Café.
5. Sherlock loves football – Fußball.
6. The café is a mess – Unordnung.
7. At the café they see the police officer – Polizeibeamter/in and Mrs Abrihim.
8. They look around – sich umsehen the café for clues.
9. Luke and Sherlock want to help – helfen Mrs Abrihim.
10. They want to solve – lösen the mystery.
11. He finds a hole – Loch. It's in the ceiling – Zimmerdecke.
12. Luke and Sherlock play football in the park – Park.

b) Put the sentences in the correct order. Bringe die Sätze in die richtige Reihenfolge.

12, 5, 4, 7, 6, 9, 10, 8, 2, 3, 11, 1

What's the word?

1. Schau, da ist ein Flamingo im Park. Das ist das erste Mal. — Look, there's a flamingo in the park. That's the first time.
2. Wir müssen ihm helfen. Lass uns mit ihm zum Zoo gehen. — We have to help it. Let's go to the zoo with it.
3. Jetzt ist es halb acht. Um Viertel nach acht haben wir Mathe. — Now it's half past seven. At quarter past eight we have Maths.
4. Dass ist nicht einfach. Aber wir schaffen das. — That's not easy but we can do it.
5. Wie können wir in den Zoo hereinkommen? — How can we get in the zoo?
6. Sie öffnen um Viertel vor acht. — They open at quarter to eight.
7. Dann können wir auch die Löwen und Kamele sehen. — Then we can see the lions and camels too.
8. Aber die Krokodile und Zebras können wir nicht sehen. Sie gehen spät ins Bett. — But we can't see the crocodiles and zebras. They go to bed late.

23 Put a circle around the odd one out. Write it in German.
Welches Wort passt nicht in die Reihe? Kreise es ein. Schreibe es auf Deutsch auf.

1. cat • (flamingo) • dog — Flamingo
2. flamingo • parrot • (lion) — Löwe
3. penguin • fish • (zebra) — Zebra
4. horse • bat • (crocodile) — Krokodil
5. plant • fruit • tree • (camel) — Kamel

24 Finish the words. Vervollständige die Wörter.

1. go to bed (ins Bett gehen)
2. the first time (das erste Mal)
3. half past (halb)
4. have to (müssen)
5. We can do it! (Wir schaffen das!)
6. quarter to (Viertel vor)
7. quarter past (Viertel nach)
8. to get in (hereinkommen)

What's the word?

1. Der Oktober ist ein besonderer Monat. — October is a _special_ month.
2. Halloween ist im Oktober. — Halloween is _in October_ .
3. Ich feiere es mit meinen Freunden. — I _celebrate_ it with my friends.
4. Wir gehen zu Häusern und sagen: „Süßes, sonst gibts Saures!" — We go to houses and say: "_Trick or treat_ _____ !"
5. Wir tragen Kostüme. — We _wear costumes_ .
6. Sie sind sehr gruselig. — They are very _scary_ .
7. Im Februar oder im März tragen wir auch Kostüme. — In _February_ or _March_ we wear costumes too.
8. Dann tragen wir eine rote Nase. — Then we wear a red _nose_ .

1 Write the months. Finde die Monate und schreibe sie auf Englisch und Deutsch auf.

1. Jneu — _June – Juni_
2. Stempbere — _September – September_
3. ebrFurya — _February – Februar_
4. yllu — _July – Juli_
5. priAl — _April – April_
6. rNovbeem — _November – November_

2 Look at the pictures and write the months in English and German. Schau dir die Bilder an und schreibe die Monate auf Englisch und Deutsch auf.

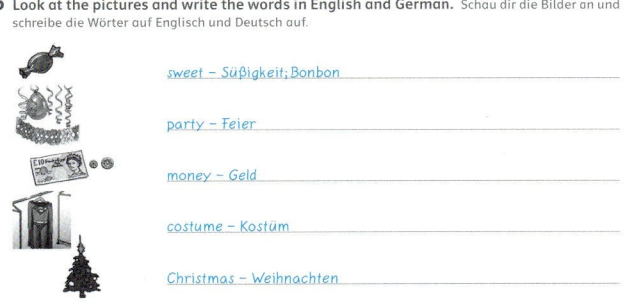

August – August

January – Januar

December – Dezember

October – Oktober

May – Mai

What's the word?

1. Meine Freunde haben kein Geld. — My friends have no _money_ .
2. Meine Freunde und ich gehen zusammen Geld sammeln. — My friends and I _collect_ money _together_ .
3. Dann tragen wir schöne Kleider und wir sehen sehr unterschiedlich aus. — Then we wear nice _clothes_ and we look very _different_ .
4. Am Abend machen wir ein Feuer. — In the _evening_ we make a _fire_ .
5. Ich bekomme Kleidung und Geld von meiner Familie. — I _get_ clothes and money from my family.
6. Meine Freundin ist eine Muslimin. — My friend is a _Muslim_ .
7. Sie feiert Eid mit ihrer Familie. — She celebrates _Eid_ with her family.

3 Complete the words. Vervollständige die Wörter mit den fehlenden Buchstaben und übersetze sie ins Deutsche.

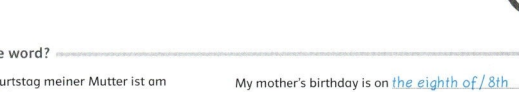

A A E E E E E E E E E I I I I I
O O O U

1. c o l e c t _sammeln_
2. c l o t h e s _Kleider_
3. sp e c i a l _besonders, speziell_
4. e v e n i n g _Abend_
5. d i f f e r e n t _unterschiedlich_
6. f i r e _Feuer_
7. c o s t u m e s _Kostüme_
8. A p r i l _April_

4 Find thirteen words.

a) Find the English words. (↓ and →) Finde die englischen Wörter.

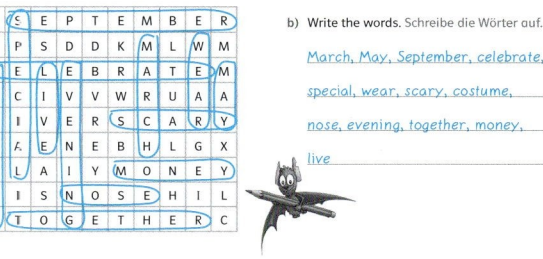

F	S	E	P	T	E	M	B	E	R
Y	P	S	D	D	K	M	L	W	M
C	E	L	E	B	R	A	T	E	M
O	C	I	V	V	W	R	U	A	A
S	I	V	E	R	S	C	A	R	Y
T	A	E	N	E	H	L	G	X	Y
U	L	A	I	Y	M	O	N	E	Y
M	I	S	N	O	S	E	H	I	L
E	T	O	G	E	T	H	E	R	C

b) Write the words. Schreibe die Wörter auf.

March, May, September, celebrate, special, wear, scary, costume, nose, evening, together, money, live

---

What's the word?

1. Im Dezember feiern wir Weihnachten zusammen. — In _December_ we celebrate _Christmas_ together.
2. Wir feiern meinen Geburtstag im April. — We celebrate my _birthday_ in April.
3. Es gibt eine kleine Feier mit meiner Familie. — There is a small _party_ with my family.
4. Und eine große Feier mit meinen Freunden. — And a _big_ party with my friends.
5. Meine Mutter kauft Süßigkeiten. — My mother buys _sweets_ .
6. An meinem Geburtstag gehe ich spät ins Bett. — On my birthday I _go to bed_ late.

5 Find the words. Write the English and German words. Finde die Wörter. Schreibe sie auf Englisch und Deutsch auf.

bigAprilsweetsbirthdaychristmasgotobedpartyfire

big – groß	_Christmas – Weihnachten_
April – April	_go to bed – ins Bett gehen_
sweets – Süßigkeiten	_party – Party; Feier_
birthday – Geburtstag	_fire – Feuer_

6 Look at the pictures and write the words in English and German. Schau dir die Bilder an und schreibe die Wörter auf Englisch und Deutsch auf.

sweet – Süßigkeit; Bonbon

party – Feier

money – Geld

costume – Kostüm

Christmas – Weihnachten

What's the word?

1. Der Geburtstag meiner Mutter ist am acht ten Februar. — My mother's birthday is on _the eighth of / 8th_ February.
2. Der Geburtstag meines Vaters ist am elften Mai. — My father's birthday is on _the eleventh of / 11th_ May.
3. 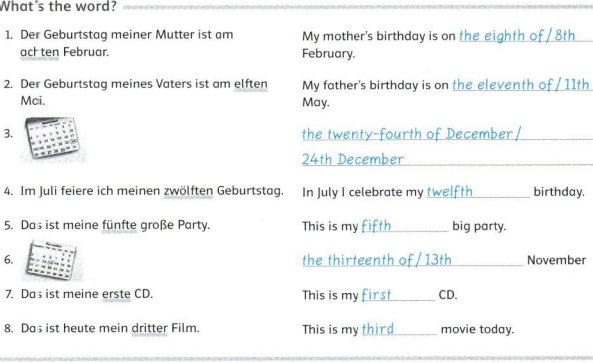 — _the twenty-fourth of December / 24th December_
4. Im Juli feiere ich meinen zwölften Geburtstag. — In July I celebrate my _twelfth_ birthday.
5. Das ist meine fünfte große Party. — This is my _fifth_ big party.
6. — _the thirteenth of / 13th_ November
7. Das ist meine erste CD. — This is my _first_ CD.
8. Das ist heute mein dritter Film. — This is my _third_ movie today.

7 Complete the numbers and the sentences. Vervollständige die Zahlen und die Sätze.

1. 1st — This is Luke's _first_ present.
2. 9th — The school is the _ninth_ house on the right.
3. _4th_ — Sam's birthday is on fourth October.
4. _24th_ — We celebrate Christmas on twenty-fourth December.
5. _13th_ — 'M' is the _thirteenth_ letter of the alphabet.

8 Look at the pictures and complete the sentences. Schaue dir das Bild an. Vervollständige die Sätze zu jeder Person.

inline skates | cap
orange sweatshirt
skateboard | green
skirt | blue jeans
red clothes | yellow T-shirt
white | black
shoes | orange
football | T-shirt
banana

1. The first person has _green_ jeans.
2. The _second_ person has _white_ shoes.
3. The _third_ person has blue jeans.
4. The _first_ boy has _orange_ shoes and has a _football_ in his hand.
5. The fourth person _(individuelle Lösung)_ .
6. _(individuelle Lösung)_

What's the word?

1. Lasst uns einen <u>Grill</u> kaufen. — Let's buy a <u>barbecue</u>.
2. Wir wollen <u>eine Grillparty</u> machen. — We want to <u>have a barbecue party</u>.
3. Wir haben <u>immer</u> Fleisch. — We <u>always</u> have meat.
4. Und <u>oft</u> haben wir Kuchen. — And we <u>often</u> have cake.
5. <u>Manchmal</u> haben wir auch Obst. — We <u>sometimes</u> have fruit too.
6. Aber wir haben <u>nie</u> Bananen. Ich mag sie nicht. — But we <u>never</u> have bananas. I don't like them.
7. Es macht immer viel Spaß. — It's always a lot of <u>fun</u>.

9 Match the word parts. Ordne die Wortteile zu. Schreibe sie auf Englisch und Deutsch auf.

al — times
par — ten
birth — ty
ne — ways
bar — day
of — ver
some — becue

<u>always – immer</u>
<u>party – Party</u>
<u>birthday – Geburtstag</u>
<u>never – nie</u>
<u>barbecue – Grill</u>
<u>often – oft</u>
<u>sometimes – manchmal</u>

10 Complete the words. Vervollständige die Wörter mit den fehlenden Buchstaben und übersetze sie ins Deutsche.

A A A A E E E E E E E I O O U U U

1. pr<u>e</u>s<u>e</u>nt <u>Geschenk</u>
2. b<u>a</u>rb<u>ecue</u> <u>Grill</u>
3. f<u>u</u>n <u>Spaß; Freude</u>
4. ch<u>o</u>col<u>a</u>t<u>e</u> <u>Schokolade</u>
5. c<u>a</u>rd <u>Karte</u>
6. c<u>u</u>t<u>e</u> <u>niedlich, süß</u>
7. c<u>a</u>k<u>e</u> <u>Kuchen</u>
8. g<u>i</u>v<u>e</u> <u>geben</u>

What's the word?

1. Es ist Halloween. Lasst uns eine <u>Verkleidungsparty</u> machen. — It's Halloween. Let's <u>have a fancy dress party</u>.
2. Die Kostüme sind eine Überraschung. — The costumes are a <u>surprise</u>.
3. Ich möchte <u>meine Freunde einladen</u>. — I want to <u>invite my friends</u>.
4. Lasst uns Karten kaufen. — Let's buy <u>cards</u>.
5. Ich möchte sie meinen Freunden geben. — I want to <u>give</u> them to my friends.
6. Ich liebe es, Geschenke zu kaufen. — I love to buy <u>presents</u>.
7. Meine Mutter kann einen Kuchen für uns backen. — My mother can <u>make a cake</u> for us.
8. Mein Hund ist auch da. Ich möchte <u>ihm</u> auch ein Kostüm kaufen. — My dog is there too. I want to buy <u>him</u> a costume too.

11 Match the sentence parts. Ordne die Satzteile zu.

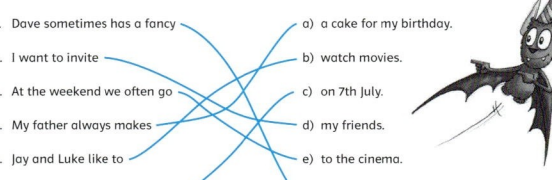

1. Dave sometimes has a fancy
2. I want to invite
3. At the weekend we often go
4. My father always makes
5. Jay and Luke like to
6. My family sometimes
7. Holly's birthday is

a) a cake for my birthday.
b) watch movies.
c) on 7th July.
d) my friends.
e) to the cinema.
f) dress party.
g) has a barbecue party.

12 Look at the pictures and write the words. Schau dir die Bilder an und schreibe die Wörter auf.

<u>card</u>
<u>cake</u>
<u>present</u>
<u>fancy dress (party), costume</u>

What's the word?

1. Am Wochenende wollen wir <u>ins Kino</u> gehen. — At the weekend we want to <u>go to the cinema</u>.
2. Wir schauen gerne <u>Filme</u>. — We like to <u>watch movies</u>.
3. Manchmal sind die Filme <u>schlecht</u>. — Sometimes the movies are <u>bad</u>.
4. Wir essen immer Schokolade. — We always eat <u>chocolate</u>.
5. — <u>date</u>
6. Mein Hund ist <u>niedlich</u>. — My dog is <u>cute</u>.
7. Ich <u>vergesse</u> den Geburtstag meiner Mutter nie. — I never <u>forget</u> my mum's birthday.

13 Put a circle around the odd one out. Write it in German.
Welches Wort passt nicht in die Reihe? Kreise es ein. Schreibe es auf Deutsch auf.

1. never · sometimes · often · (him) — <u>ihm, ihn</u>
2. (fun) · forget · get · give — <u>Spaß; Freude</u>
3. nut · (barbecue) · chocolate · banana — <u>Grill</u>
4. present · cake · (elephant) · card — <u>Elefant</u>
5. good · nice · great · (bad) — <u>schlecht</u>
6. second · third · (forget) · fifth — <u>vergessen</u>
7. barbecue · fire · meat · (cute) — <u>niedlich</u>
8. (surprise) · sweet · chocolate · cake — <u>Überraschung</u>

14 Look at the pictures and complete the sentences. Schau dir die Bilder an und vervollständige die Sätze.

1. Dave always gives Holly a <u>present</u>.
2. I always <u>invite</u> all my friends to my birthday party.
3. We often eat <u>chocolate</u> at birthday parties.
4. I sometimes <u>go to the cinema</u> with my friends.
5. Or we <u>watch movies</u> on TV at home.

What's the word?

1. Ich liebe Einkaufen. — I love <u>shopping</u>.
2. Wir gehen immer in den Tante-Emma-Laden. — We always go to the <u>corner shop</u>.
3. Wir kaufen dort einige Dinge. — We buy <u>some</u> <u>things</u> there.
4. Was kann ich für dich tun? — <u>How can I help you</u>?
5. Wir brauchen Sachen für meinen Geburtstag. — We <u>need</u> things for my birthday.
6. — <u>balloon</u>
7. — two <u>candles</u>
8. — <u>box</u>
9. Darf es sonst noch etwas sein? — <u>Anything else</u>?
10. — <u>a bar of chocolate</u>

15 Put in the right words. Setze die richtigen Wörter ein.

else · can · forget · of · need · some

Mr Benn: Hello. How <u>can</u> I help you?
Dave: I <u>need</u> two pencils and <u>some</u> things for my birthday.
Mr Benn: OK, here you are. Anything <u>else</u>?
Dave: Yes, a bar <u>of</u> chocolate, please. I never <u>forget</u> chocolate!

16 Write the words. Finde die Wörter und schreibe sie auf Englisch und Deutsch auf.

1. aeslndc <u>candles – Kerzen</u>
2. rba fo lactecoho <u>bar of chocolate – Tafel Schokolade</u>
3. xbo <u>box – Schachtel</u>
4. sgtnhi <u>things – Sachen; Dinge</u>
5. eden <u>need – brauchen</u>
6. etfrgo <u>forget – vergessen</u>

What's the word?

1. Lass uns zehn Eier und Zucker kaufen.
Let's buy ten _eggs_ and _sugar_ .

2. Brauchen wir auch Milch?
Do we need _milk_ too?

3. Ich muss auf meinen Einkaufszettel schauen.
I have to look at my _shopping list_ .

4. Nein, aber wir brauchen Schokolade und Butter.
No, but we need chocolate and _butter_ .

5. Okay. Ich brauche auch Käse für ein belegtes Brot.
OK. I need _cheese_ for a _sandwich_ too.

6. Lass uns Orangen kaufen.
Let's buy _oranges_ .

7. Und wir brauchen Chips und Cola für die Party.
And we need _crisps_ and _coke_ for the party.

17 Write a list. Schreibe die Einkaufsliste für das Rezept auf Englisch.

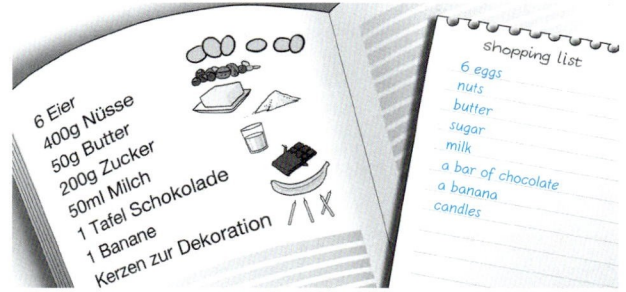

6 Eier
400g Nüsse
50g Butter
200g Zucker
50ml Milch
1 Tafel Schokolade
1 Banane
Kerzen zur Dekoration

shopping list
6 eggs
nuts
butter
sugar
milk
a bar of chocolate
a banana
candles

18 Cross the odd ones out. Streiche die Wörter durch, die nicht zur Party passen.

~~bad surprise~~ • sandwiches • chocolate • balloon • ~~river~~ • cake • ~~space~~ • candles • crisps •
coke • sweets • ~~sandwiches~~ • costumes • friends • fun

What's the word?

1. Wie viel kostet diese Tafel Schokolade?
How much is this bar of chocolate?

2. Sie kostet 99 Pence.
It _is 99p_ .

3. Ich brauche eine Flasche Cola.
I need a _bottle_ of coke.

4. Entschuldigung, könntest du das bitte wiederholen?
Sorry, can you say that again, please ?

5. Ich brauche auch eine Packung Zucker.
I need a _packet_ of sugar too.

6. Wie bitte?
Pardon ?

7. Wir haben keine CDs. Es tut mir leid.
We don't have _CDs_ . I'm sorry

8. Ist das alles? Das macht 2 Pfund und 24 Pence.
That's all? _That's £2.24_ .

9. Hier ist dein Wechselgeld. – Dankeschön.
Here's your change . – Thank you.

10. Gern geschehen.
You're welcome .

19 Match the sentence parts. Ordne die Satzteile zu.

1. How — b) much is the sugar?
2. Sorry, can you — f) say that again, please?
3. Anything — e) else?
4. Where are the — c) eggs?
5. You're — a) welcome.
6. Here's your — d) change.
7. I need a bar — g) of chocolate.
8. How can I — j) help you?
9. The pencils — h) are 99 p.
10. I — k) am sorry.
11. That's — i) £5.46.

What's the word?

1. Das ist die Einladung für meine Freunde.
This is the _invitation_ for my friends.

2. Jeder bekommt eine. Ich gebe sie ihnen.
Everyone gets one. I give it to _them_ .

3. Ich denke, die Einladung ist gut.
I _think_ the invitation is good.

4. Ich frage meine Freunde.
I _ask_ my friends.

5. Sie sagen, sie ist toll.
They say it's _brilliant_ .

6. Alles Gute zum Geburtstag!
Happy birthday !

7. Lasst uns ins Haus hineingehen.
Let's go _into_ the house.

20 Find the words. Write the English and German words.
Finde die Wörter. Schreibe sie auf Englisch und Deutsch auf.

thinkinvitationeveryonehappybirthdaybrilliantintothemask

think – denken, glauben   invitation – Einladung
everyone – jeder   Happy birthday! – Alles Gute zum Geburtstag!
brilliant – toll   into – in; hinein
them – sie   ask – fragen

21 Right or wrong?
Read the text on pages 80/81 in your book. Are the sentences right or wrong? Tick ✔ the right box.
Lies den Text auf Seite 80/81 im Buch. Sind die Sätze richtig oder falsch? Kreuze ✔ on.

	right	wrong
1. There is a birthday party at Jay's house.	✔	
2. There are nine people at the party.		✔
3. Luke is the pirate.		✔
4. Jay's mum wants to take a photo.	✔	
5. There is water on the table.		✔
6. Dave's costume is green.		✔
7. Olivia comes to the party late.	✔	
8. Olivia and Jay dance.		✔

What's the word?

1. Ich liebe Karneval.
I love _carnival_ .

2.
witch

3. Luke ist der beste Tänzer.
Luke is the best _dancer_ .

4.
Superman

5. Ich möchte ein Foto machen.
I want to _take a photo_ .

6.
alien

7. Schlümpfe sind blau und weiß.
Smurfs are blue and white.

8.
pirate

9. Ich bin eine Hexe. Sei vorsichtig!
I'm a witch. _Be careful_ !

22 Write the word pairs. Schreibe die Wortpaare auf.

[ask] [invitation] [them] [think] [everyone] [brilliant]

1. all – _everyone_   4. party – _invitation_
2. ? – _ask_   5. ◯ – _think_
3. great – _brilliant_   6. they – _them_

23 Find six costumes.

a) Find the English words. (↓ und →) Finde die englischen Wörter.

N	D	C	D	N	U	X	A
P	I	R	A	T	E	V	L
F	S	Y	N	R	W	O	I
C	M	T	C	B	H	P	E
S	U	P	E	R	M	A	N
L	R	N	R	J	K	L	U
M	F	T	W	I	T	C	H

b) Write the words in English and German. Schreibe die Wörter auf Deutsch und Englisch auf.

pirate – Pirat(in); Seeräuber(in)   dancer – Tänzer(in)

Superman – Supermann   alien – Außerirdischer

smurf – Schlumpf   witch – Hexe

What's the word?

1. Lieber Luke, ... — <u>Dear</u> Luke, ...
2. — <u>drums</u>
3. Meine Übernachtungsparty ist am Samstag. — My <u>sleepover</u> is on Saturday.
4. Es gibt verschiedene Snacks. — There are different <u>snacks</u>.
5. Es gibt viele verschiedene Nachspeisen. — There are <u>lots of</u> different <u>desserts</u>.
6. Meine Freunde mögen den Kuchen am liebsten. — My friends <u>like</u> the cake <u>best</u>.
7. Wir singen auch Karaoke auf der Party. — We sing <u>karaoke</u> at the party too.

24 Put in the missing words. Setze die fehlenden Wörter ein.

D<u>ear</u> Holly,

This is an <u>invitation</u> to my s<u>leepover</u>. It's next Saturday.

We want to sing k<u>araoke</u> and we always eat l<u>ots of</u> different sn<u>acks</u>.

Do you know carrot pudding?

It's a d<u>essert</u>. I like it b<u>est</u>.

See you, Luke

25 Match the words. Ordne die passenden Wörter richtig zu.

1. brilliant
2. say
3. dessert
4. snack
5. invitation
6. barbecue
7. third
8. hundredth
9. second
10. packet

a) carrot pudding
b) box
c) great
d) 3rd
e) ask
f) sandwich
g) 100th
h) 2nd
i) meat
j) card

What's the word?

1. Es ist Samstag. Lasst uns ein Picknick im Park machen. — It's Saturday. Let's <u>have a picnic in the park</u>.
2. Nein, ich möchte in einen Freizeitpark gehen. — No, I want <u>to go to a theme park</u>.
3. Okay. Lasst uns zuerst in ein Fastfood-Restaurant gehen. — OK. Let's <u>go to a fast food restaurant</u> first.
4. Dort will ich mein Lieblingsessen genießen. — I want to <u>have my favourite meal</u> there.
5. Ich mag Hamburger am liebsten. — I like <u>burgers</u> best.
6. Und ich mag Eis mit Erdbeeren. — And I like <u>ice cream</u> with <u>strawberries</u>.
7. Jay möchte eine Übernachtungsparty machen. — Jay wants to <u>have a sleepover</u>.

26 Translate the words and talk about you. Übersetze die Wörter und erzähle über dich. Setze die passenden Wörter ein.

[never] [sometimes] [often] [always]

sonntags • Filme schauen
<u>On Sundays I often watch movies.</u>

1. im Januar • ein Picknick im Park machen.
<u>In January I (individuelle Lösung) have a picnic in the park.</u>

2. an Wochenenden • in einen Freizeitpark gehen
<u>At weekends I (individuelle Lösung) go to a theme park.</u>

3. in der Cafeteria • ein Lieblingsessen genießen
<u>I (individuelle Lösung) have my favourite meal in the cafeteria.</u>

4. mit meinen Freunden • in ein Fastfood-Restaurant gehen
<u>I (individuelle Lösung) go to a fast food restaurant with my friends.</u>

5. mittwochs • eine Übernachtungsparty machen
<u>On Wednesdays I (individuelle Lösung) have a sleepover.</u>

What's the word?

1. Lass uns einkaufen gehen. Wir brauchen Pfirsiche und Limonade. — Let's go shopping. We need <u>peaches</u> and <u>lemonade</u>.
2. Okay. Lass uns die Dose nehmen. — OK. Let's take the <u>can</u>.
3. Wir brauchen Mehl für den Kuchen. — We need <u>flour</u> for the cake.
4.  — <u>biscuits</u>
5. — <u>pasta</u>
6. Die anderen und ich sind auf einer Verkleidungsparty. — <u>The others</u> and I are at a fancy dress party.
7. Ich bin ein Außerirdischer. Hast du Angst? — I'm an alien. <u>Are</u> you <u>scared</u>?
8. Natürlich habe ich keine Angst. — <u>Of course</u> I'm not scared.
9. — <u>dance</u>
10. Dave läutet die Türklingel, aber niemand hört es. — Dave <u>rings</u> the <u>doorbell</u>, but no one <u>hears</u> it.
11. Der Erzähler der Geschichte ist ein Junge. — The <u>narrator</u> of the story is a boy.

27 Put a circle around the odd one out. Write it in German.
Welches Wort passt nicht in die Reihe? Kreise es ein. Schreibe es auf Deutsch auf.

1. peach • orange • strawberry • (pasta) — <u>Nudeln</u>
2. (biscuit) • coke • lemonade • milk — <u>Keks</u>
3. sugar • (burger) • flour • butter — <u>Hamburger</u>
4. ice cream • cake • (peach) • chocolate — <u>Pfirsich</u>

28 Write the words. Finde die Wörter und schreibe sie auf Englisch und Deutsch auf.

1. lobolerd — <u>doorbell – Türklingel</u>
2. eb radsce — <u>be scared – Angst haben</u>
3. necad — <u>dance – Tanz; tanzen</u>
4. nirg — <u>ring – läuten; klingeln</u>
5. teh sohert — <u>the others – die anderen</u>
6. reha — <u>hear – hören</u>

What's the word?

1. Unsere Wohnung hat zwei Schlafzimmer. — Our <u>flat</u> has two bedrooms.
2. Wohnen deine Freunde in deiner Straße? — Do your friends live in your <u>road</u>?
3. Wir haben ein Haus mit einem Garten. — We have a <u>house</u> with a garden.
4. Samstags spielen wir Fußball im Park. — On Saturdays we play football in the <u>park</u>.
5. Die Cutty Sark ist ein berühmtes Schiff. — The Cutty Sark is a famous <u>ship</u>.
6. Redditch ist eine schöne Stadt. — Redditch is a nice <u>town</u>.
7. Wir haben ein Schwimmbad an unserer Schule. — We have a <u>swimming pool</u> at our school.
8. Lass uns ein Sandwich im Café essen. — Let's have a sandwich in the <u>café</u>.

1 Look at the picture and write the words. Schau dir das Bild an und schreibe die Wörter auf.

6 It's a nice <u>town</u>.

❶ <u>café</u>
❷ <u>road</u>
❸ <u>house</u>
❹ <u>park</u>
❺ <u>ship</u>
❼ <u>swimming pool</u>
❽ <u>flat</u>

2 Complete the crossword and find another word.
Vervollständige das Kreuzworträtsel und finde das Lösungswort.

1. Dave lives in a ....
2. Pirates live on a ....
3. Buses go on ....
4. There's a playground in Greenwich ....
5. I love our swimming ....
6. Luke and Holly live in ....
7. Greenwich is a famous old ....
8. ... is the eighth month of the year.

What's the word? <u>S H O P P I N G</u>

Crossword grid:
- 1 across: H O U S E
- 2 down: S R I A
- 3: R A O
- 4 down: W W O
- 5 down: W U C
- S H O P P I N G
- 6 down: G R E E N
- 7: E T N O
- 8: A U

What's the word?

1. Was können wir in diesem <u>Laden</u> kaufen?   What can we buy in this <u>shop</u> ?

2. ↔ <u>new</u>   The *Cutty Sark* is an <u>old</u> ship.

3. Man kann Fußbälle im <u>Sportgeschäft</u> kaufen.   You can buy footballs in a <u>sports shop</u> .

4. Wo ist das <u>Postamt</u>?   Where is the <u>post office</u> ?

5. Das Postamt ist im <u>Einkaufszentrum</u>.   The post office is in the <u>shopping centre</u> .

6. Ich <u>gehe</u> Sonntag morgens <u>schwimmen</u>.   I <u>go swimming</u> on Sunday mornings.

3 Where can you find the things in the pictures? Schaue dir die Bilder an und schreibe auf, wo man diese Dinge finden kann.

<u>s p o r t s   s h o p</u>   <u>p o s t   o f f i c e</u>   <u>s h i p</u>   <u>s w i m m i n g   p o o l</u>

<u>h o u s e</u> / <u>f l a t</u>   <u>p a r k</u>   <u>t o w n</u>   <u>c a f é</u>

4 Put in the right words. Setze die richtigen Wörter ein.

| pool | museum | town | house | café | swimming | park |

Luke lives in a <u>house</u> in Greenwich. Greenwich is a famous, old <u>town</u> in London. It has a big <u>park</u> , and Luke often takes his dog, Sherlock, there. There's a <u>museum</u> about time with some old clocks and a café in the park. Luke often eats a sandwich in the <u>café</u> . There's also a swimming <u>pool</u> in Greenwich, and Luke often goes <u>swimming</u> there with Dave or other friends.

What's the word?

1. Ich frühstücke jeden Morgen.   I eat breakfast every <u>morning</u> .

2. Es ist Montag. <u>Gestern</u> war Sonntag.   It's Monday. <u>Yesterday</u> was Sunday.

3. Ich bin müde und ich will ins Bett gehen.   I'm <u>tired</u> and I want to go to bed.

4. Luke: Fußball ist immer spannend.   Luke: Football is always <u>exciting</u> .

5. Weißt du was? Heute habe ich Geburtstag.   <u>Guess what</u> ? It's my birthday.

6. Gefallen dir meine neuen <u>Turnschuhe</u>?   Do you like my new <u>trainers</u> ?

7. Letzte Woche kam ein guter Film im Fernsehen.   There was a good film on TV <u>last</u> week.

8.   I love <u>pizza</u> .

9. Ich mache meine Hausaufgaben in der Küche.   I <u>do</u> my <u>homework</u> in the kitchen.

10. Ich bin jetzt sehr glücklich.   I'm very <u>happy</u> now.

5 Complete the Crossword.

a) Complete the crossword. Vervollständige das Kreuzworträtsel.

Down ▼:
1. There's a ... pool in Greenwich.
2. You need these for sport.
4. It's 15th August now. ... was the 14th.
6. We often eat ... in the cafeteria at school.

Across ▶:
3. Why are you ...? – I went to bed late.
5. Some films are very ... .
7. School starts at 9:00 in the ... .
8. 31st December is the ... day of the year.
9. A new phone? I'm really ... for you!

3 ▶ T I R E D
5 ▶ E X C I T I N G
7 ▶ M O R N I N G
8 ▶ L A S T   9 ▶ H A P P Y

Down: SWIMMING, TRAINERS, YESTERDAY, PIZZA

b) Make a word from the letters in the blue boxes. Bilde ein Wort aus den Buchstaben in den blauen Kästchen.

What's the word?
Something you like to drink: <u>lemonade</u>

What's the word?

1. <u>Gestern</u> war Daves Geburtstag.   Yesterday it <u>was</u> Dave's birthday.

2. Wir haben das Spiel am Samstag gewonnen.   We <u>won</u> the game on Saturday.

3. Gestern habe ich eine berühmte Person gesehen.   I <u>saw</u> a famous person yesterday.

4. Luke hat ein Sandwich in dem Café gekauft.   Luke <u>bought</u> a sandwich in the café.

5. Am Montag bist du früh nach Hause gegangen.   You <u>went</u> home early on Monday.

6. Luke hatte gestern Fußballtraining.   Luke <u>had</u> football practice yesterday.

7. Sie haben ihre Hausaufgaben in der Schule gemacht.   They <u>did</u> their homework at school.

8. Erzähl mir bitte eine Geschichte.   <u>Tell</u> me a story, please.

6 Put in the right verb forms. Setze die richtigen Verbformen ein.

infinitive	simple past	German
to tell	told	erzählen
to be	was, were	sein
to have	had	haben
to buy	bought	kaufen
to go	went	gehen
to see	saw	sehen
to win	won	gewinnen

7 One sentence part is right. Put a circle around it. Kreise die richtigen Satzteile ein.

1. Amina went (to the shops.) / new trainers. / happy.

2. Ken bought at the sports shop. / (a new T-shirt.) / on Saturday.

3. Sue told me pizza. / (a story.) / money.

4. Daniel's party was to a café. / a good friend. / (at his house.)

What's the word?

1. Ich fahre mit dem <u>Fahrrad</u> zur Schule.   I go to school by <u>bike</u> .

2. Wir fahren immer mit dem <u>Bus</u> in die Stadt.   We always go to town by <u>bus</u> .

3. Wir haben ein neues deutsches <u>Auto</u>.   We have a new German <u>car</u> .

4. Mein Onkel hat ein altes <u>Schiff</u>.   My uncle has an old <u>ship</u> .

5. Ich gehe gern im <u>Meer</u> schwimmen.   I like to go swimming in the <u>sea</u> .

6. Und ich spiele gern Volleyball am <u>Strand</u>.   And I like to play volleyball on the <u>beach</u> .

7. Unser Hund liebt es, <u>Frisbee</u> zu spielen.   Our dog loves to play <u>frisbee</u> .

8. Nach dem <u>Ausflug</u> waren wir sehr müde.   After the trip we <u>were</u> very tired.

9. Meine Oma wohnt <u>am Meer</u>.   My grandma lives <u>at the seaside</u> .

10. Meine Oma machte einen <u>Ausflug</u> nach London.   My grandma went on a <u>trip</u> to London.

11. Es gibt einen <u>Zug</u> von London nach Paris.   There's a <u>train</u> from London to Paris.

12.   I like to get <u>postcards</u> from friends.

13. Man isst oft <u>Pommes</u> in England.   You often eat <u>chips</u> in England.

8 Find eight words.

a) Find the English words. (↓ and →) Finde die englischen Wörter.

C	L	P	L	C	H
B	E	A	C	H	L
Y	T	F	E	X	P
M	R	V	C	A	R
C	A	B	T	C	T
B	I	K	E	H	S
V	N	G	A	I	H
S	E	A	M	P	I
U	N	B	U	S	P

b) Write the words in English and German. Schreibe die Wörter auf Englisch und Deutsch auf.

<u>beach – Strand</u>
<u>bike – Fahrrad</u>
<u>chips – Pommes</u>
<u>car – Auto</u>
<u>sea – Meer</u>
<u>bus – Bus</u>
<u>train – Zug</u>
<u>ship – Schiff</u>

What's the word?

1. Wir gehen immer zu Fuß in die Stadt.
We always go to town on foot.

2. Kann man nach London laufen? – Nein, es ist zwei Stunden von hier entfernt.
Can you walk to London? – No, it's two hours from here.

3. Wir können mit dem Zug fahren.
We can go by train.

4. London ist groß und ich verirre mich oft dort.
London is big and I often get lost there.

5. Wir haben uns verirrt. – Oje.
We got lost. – Oh dear.

6. Wir finden den Weg mit unserem Navi.
We find our way with our satnav.

7. Bringe bitte das Buch auf dem Weg nach Hause mit.
Please get the book on the way home.

8. Es tut mir leid. Ich habe das Buch vergessen.
Sorry, I forgot the book.

9. Ich bin Vegetarier. Ich esse kein Fleisch.
I'm a vegetarian. I don't eat meat.

10. Die Pommes sind kalt. Ich kann sie nicht essen.
The chips are cold. I can't eat them.

11. Ich möchte meine Postkarten verschicken.
I want to send my postcards.

9 Find the words and put them in. Finde die Wörter heraus und setze sie ein.

| asseeid | carostpd | dens | prit | slot | morf | yb | antsav |

Ben: We went to my uncle's house last week. He lives at the seaside.

Lizzy: Oh, I didn't get your postcard.

Ben: I didn't send you a postcard. We were only there for three days.

Lizzy: Oh, did you have a good trip?

Ben: No, we didn't. We got lost. Margate is only three hours from here, but we needed six hours.

Lizzy: Why didn't you go by train?

Ben: My dad wanted to go by car because he has a new satnav.

What's the word?

1. Sie sprechen Englisch in Australien.
They speak English in Australia.

2. Dieser Mann ist aus Australien.
This man is from Australia.

3. Es gibt schöne Strände in Australien.
There are beautiful beaches in Australia.

4.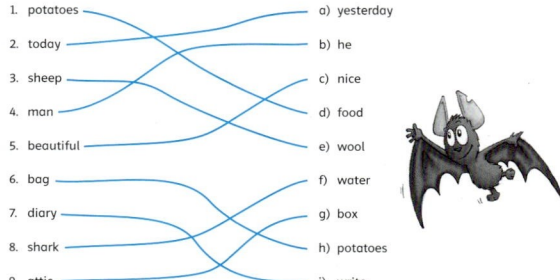
Don't go swimming with a shark.

5. Ich mag Haie nicht. Sie sind furchtbar.
I don't like sharks. They are awful.

6. Ich bin sehr hungrig. Ich will Kartoffeln essen.
I'm very hungry. I want to eat potatoes.

7. Dann lass uns heute einen Sack Kartoffeln kaufen.
Then let's buy a bag of potatoes today.

8. Wir haben Kisten auf dem Dachboden.
We have boxes in our attic.

9. Mein altes Tagebuch ist auch auf dem Dachboden.
My old diary is in the attic too.

10.
Sheep eat grass.

11. Man bekommt Wolle von Schafen.
You get wool from sheep.

12. Meine Großeltern hatten ein interessantes Leben, aber mein Leben ist langweilig!
My grandparents had interesting lives, but my life is boring!

10 Match the word pairs. Ordne die Wortpaare richtig zu

1. potatoes — a) yesterday
2. today — b) he
3. sheep — c) nice
4. man — d) food
5. beautiful — e) wool
6. bag — f) water
7. diary — g) box
8. shark — h) potatoes
9. attic — i) write

What's the word?

1. Ist deine Mutter zuhause? – Nein, sie ist heute unterwegs.
Is your mum at home? – No, she's out and about today.

2. Ich esse immer Popcorn im Kino.
I always eat popcorn in the cinema.

3. Entschuldigung, ist hier in der Nähe ein Postamt?
Excuse me, is there a post office near here?

4. Dein Fahrrad ist fertig. – Oh gut. Aber kann ich später nochmal wiederkommen?
Your bike is ready. – Oh good. But can I come back for it later?

5. Klar! Wann kannst du kommen?
Sure! What time can you come?

11 Where are they?

a) Match the sentence parts. Ordne die Satzteile zu.

1. Can I come — a) from here.
2. Excuse — b) his way here.
3. He's out and — c) back for it later?
4. That's — d) what?
5. But that's two hours — e) about in Margate.
6. Guess — f) at the seaside.
7. He's on — g) me.

b) Complete the text with the sentences from above. You don't need one of them.
Vervollständige den Text mit den Sätzen von oben. Ein Satz bleibt übrig.

A. At school

Student's dad: Excuse me. Where's Mr Potter, please?

English teacher: The Geography teacher? He's out and about in Margate

Student's dad: Margate? That's at the seaside

English teacher: Yes, that's right. He's on a school trip with class 7a.

Student's dad: But that's two hours from here.

English teacher: Yes, two hours by car. But it's only an hour from here by train.

B. At the music shop

Lucy: Guess what? Ray-B's in town.

George: Who's he?

Lucy: Ah, you know. He's a famous singer. He's on his way here.

What's the word?

1.
Turn right into Crane Street.

2. Kannst du mir bitte sagen, wie man zum Strand kommt?
Can you tell me the way to the beach, please?

3. Gehe geradeaus und biege links ab.
Walk straight on and turn left.

4. Das Krankenhaus ist auf der linken Seite.
The hospital is on the left.

5. Gehe geradeaus und das Café ist auf der rechten Seite.
Go straight on and the café is on the right.

6. Das Postamt ist gegenüber von dem Laden.
The post office is opposite.

7. Unser Haus ist am Ende der Straße.
Our house is at the end of the road.

12 Look at the pictures and complete the sentences. Schaue dir die Bilder an und vervollständige die Sätze.

❶
Walk straight on and turn left into London Road.

❷
The swimming pool is at the end of the road.

❸
Walk straight on and the corner shop is on the left!

❹
The post office is on the right.

❺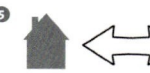
The sports shop is opposite the cinema.

❻
Can you tell me the way to the beach, please? – Yes, turn right into Margate Road and the beach is at the end of the road.

What's the word?

1. Nach dem Weg fragen ist nicht immer leicht. — _Asking the way_ isn't always easy.
2. Viele Touristen besuchen Margate jedes Jahr. — Lots of _tourists_ visit Margate every year.
3. Wo ist die Touristeninformation, bitte? — Where's the _Tourist Information Centre_, please?
4. Ich laufe gern am Strand entlang. — I love to walk _along_ the beach.
5. Mein Vater arbeitet in einem Krankenhaus. — My dad works in a _hospital_.
6. Meine Mama arbeitet bis 8 Uhr. — My mum works _until_ 8 o'clock.

13 Put a circle around the odd one out. Write it in German. Welches Wort passt nicht in die Reihe? Kreise es ein. Schreibe es auf Deutsch auf.

1. opposite • (hospital) • along • left — _Krankenhaus_
2. man • tourist • (ship) • child — _Schiff_
3. (asking the way) • Tourist information Centre • post office • swimming pool — _nach dem Weg fragen_
4. on the left • on the right • (out and about) • opposite — _unterwegs_
5. hungry • awful • beautiful • (until) — _bis_

14 Complete the sentences. Start at "You are here". Schau dir die Karte an und vervollständige die Sätze. Starte am Punkt „You are here".

Tourist 1: Can you _tell me the way_ to the cinema, please?

Henry: Sure. _Turn right_ into King Street and it's _on the left_. It's _opposite_ the restaurant.

Tourist 2: _Excuse_ me. _Can you tell me the way_ to the zoo, please?

Henry: Yes. Go _along_ Station Road and then _turn left_ into Park Street. It's _on the left_ and it's _opposite_ the school.

What's the word?

1. In der Bücherei findet man viele Bücher. — You can find lots of books at the _library_.
2. Im Kaufhaus kann man viele verschiedene Sachen kaufen. — At the _department store_ you can buy lots of different things.
3. Wir kaufen immer Obst und Käse auf dem Markt. — We always buy fruit and cheese at the _market_.
4. Es gibt ein Museum über Schiffe in London. — There's a _museum_ about ships in London.
5. Gehe nicht im Fluss schwimmen. Er ist sehr kalt. — Don't go swimming in the _river_. It's very cold.
6. Ich muss um 5 Uhr am Bahnhof sein. — I must be at the _station_ at 5 o'clock.
7. Meine Eltern fahren mit dem Auto zum Supermarkt. — My parents go to the _supermarket_ by car.

15 Read the dialogues and write the places. Lies die Dialoge und schreibe auf, wo sich die Personen befinden.

They are …

Mrs Smith:	Excuse me. Where is the sugar, please?	in a supermarket.
Mr Johnson:	It's on a shelf at the back of the shop. I can show you if you like.	
Tina:	Oh, no! We're late. The train goes in five minutes. Excuse me. Where does the train to London go from?	at a station.
Sam:	It's just over there. You have lots of time.	
Ms Adams:	Can I help you?	in a department store.
Luke:	Yes. Can you tell me where the T-shirts are?	
Ms Adams:	Yes, of course. They're there – just behind the shoes.	
Mr Baker:	Can I take these books home, please?	in a library.
Ms Evans:	Do you have your card?	
Mr Baker:	Er … no.	
Ms Evans:	Then I'm sorry. You can look at them here, but you can't take them with you.	
Mrs Miller:	I never buy fruit in a supermarket. It's much better here.	at a market.
Sally:	Yes, but Mum, it's cold here.	

What's the word?

1. U-Boote fahren im Meer. — _Submarines_ go under the sea.
2. Eine Straßenbahn ist ein Zug. Sie fährt auf der Straße. — A _tram_ is a train. It goes on the road.
3. Menschen fliegen mit dem Flugzeug nach Australien. — People go to Australia by _plane_.
4. Ein Schiff ist ein großes Boot. — A ship is a big _boat_.
5. Hubschrauber bringen Menschen ins Krankenhaus. — _Helicopters_ take people to hospital.
6. Mein Vater hat ein Motorrad. — My dad has a _motorbike_.
7. Die Londoner U-Bahn ist sehr alt. — The _underground_ in London is very old.
8. Möchtest du nach London fahren? — _Would you like_ to go to London?
9. Ich möchte jetzt gern ein Eis essen. — _I'd like to_ eat an ice cream now.
10. Ich mag mein 🛹 — I like my _skateboard_.

16 Look at the pictures and write the words. Schau dir die Bilder an und schreibe die Wörter auf.

helicopter   _underground_   _motorbike_   _boat_

submarine   _plane_   _tram_   _bike_

17 Find the words. Write the English and German words. Finde die Wörter. Schreibe sie auf Englisch und Deutsch auf.

skateboardwouldyoulikeundergroundI'dliketotramplane

skateboard – Skateboard   _I'd like to … – ich möchte …_

would you like – möchtest du   _tram – Straßenbahn_

underground – U-Bahn   _plane – Flugzeug_

What's the word?

1. Wir hatten gestern abend ein tolles Abenteuer. — We had a great _adventure_ last night.
2. Mein Ururopa war berühmt. — My _great-great-grandad_ was famous.
3. Mein Bruder hat einen Job in einem Laden. — My brother has a _job_ in a shop.
4. ⟷ love — I _hate_ homework!
5. Meine Schwester übergibt sich oft im Auto. — My sister _is_ often _sick_ in the car.
6. Mein Onkel war letztes Jahr erster Offizier, aber jetzt ist er Kapitän. — My uncle was _first mate_ last year but now he's the captain.
7. Der Sturm gestern Nacht war sehr schlimm. — The _storm_ last night was very bad.
8. Wellen sind in einem Sturm immer sehr hoch. — _Waves_ are always very high in a storm.

18 Put a circle around the odd one out. Write it in German. Welches Wort passt nicht in die Reihe? Kreise es ein. Schreibe es auf Deutsch auf.

1. first mate • (great-great-granddad) • captain — _Ururopa_
2. (hate) • love • like — _hassen_
3. storm • waves • (job) — _Job_

19 Complete the crossword. Vervollständige das Kreuzworträtsel.

Across ▶ :

1. You can put things in a … .
3. Some people write in a … every day.
5. I really don't like fish – I … it.
6. We love to play in the … in the sea.
7. My sister is always … in the car.
9. I want … fish for dinner.
10. My uncle isn't the captain, but he's the … .

Down ▼ :

2. My bedroom is under the … .
4. An … story is always exciting.
8. There's a lot of wind. It's a … .

What's the word?

1. Hast du den <u>Schrei</u> gehört? — Did you hear that <u>shout</u>?
2. „Hilfe! Hilfe! <u>Mann über Bord!</u>" — "Help! Help! <u>Man overboard</u>!"
3. Man braucht viele <u>Seile</u> auf Schiffen. — You need a lot of <u>ropes</u> on ships.
4. Ich bin hungrig, <u>deshalb</u> will ich jetzt essen. — I'm hungry <u>so</u> I want to eat now.
5. Ich hatte <u>viele</u> Pommes zum Mittagessen. — I had <u>a lot of</u> chips for lunch.

20 Put in the right words. Setz die richtigen Wörter ein.

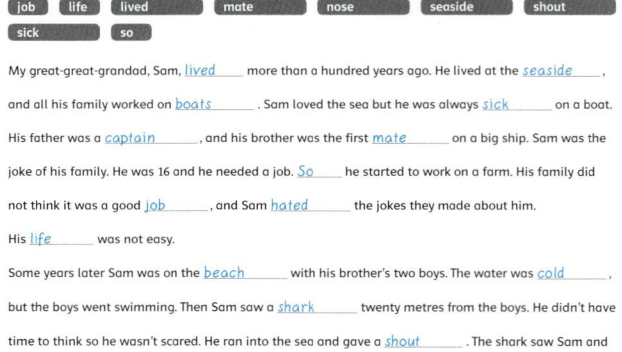

> beach · boats · captain · cold · hated · shark · job · life · lived · mate · nose · seaside · shout · sick · so

My great-great-grandad, Sam, <u>lived</u> more than a hundred years ago. He lived at the <u>seaside</u>, and all his family worked on <u>boats</u>. Sam loved the sea but he was always <u>sick</u> on a boat. His father was a <u>captain</u>, and his brother was the first <u>mate</u> on a big ship. Sam was the joke of his family. He was 16 and he needed a job. <u>So</u> he started to work on a farm. His family did not think it was a good <u>job</u>, and Sam <u>hated</u> the jokes they made about him. His <u>life</u> was not easy.

Some years later Sam was on the <u>beach</u> with his brother's two boys. The water was <u>cold</u>, but the boys went swimming. Then Sam saw a <u>shark</u> twenty metres from the boys. He didn't have time to think so he wasn't scared. He ran into the sea and gave a <u>shout</u>. The shark saw Sam and went for him. Sam hit (schlug) the shark on its <u>nose</u> and Sam and the two boys were OK. After that Sam was famous in their town and all the jokes were about the sharks.

21 Write the words. Finde die Wörter und schreibe sie auf Englisch und Deutsch auf.

1. soper <u>ropes – Seile</u>
2. naM beroovdar <u>Man overboard! – Mann über Bord!</u>
3. tusoh <u>shout – Schrei</u>
4. a tol fo <u>a lot of – viel, eine Menge</u>

What's the word?

1. Man kann Milch und Eier auf einem <u>Bauernhof</u> kaufen. — You can buy eggs and milk on a <u>farm</u>.
2. Einige <u>Bauern</u> wohnen auf Bauernhöfen. — Some <u>farmers</u> live on farms.
3. Ich bin die <u>Tochter</u> meines Vaters. — I'm my dad's <u>daughter</u>.
4. Man bekommt Eier von <u>Hühnern</u>. — You get eggs from <u>chickens</u>.
5. Unser Hund trägt immer ein <u>Halsband</u>. — Our dog always wears a <u>collar</u>.
6. Und unsere Schafe haben GPS-<u>Halsbänder</u>. — And our sheep have <u>GPS</u> collars.
7. — Farmers have two or three <u>tractors</u>.
8. Wir gehen in den Ferien oft <u>klettern</u>. — We often go <u>rock climbing</u> in the holidays.
9. Im Winter kann man im Schwimmbad <u>Kanufahren</u> gehen. — In the winter you can go <u>canoeing</u> in the swimming pool.

1 Complete the crossword. Vervollständige das Kreuzworträtsel.

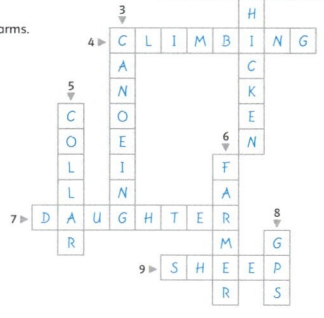

Across ▶ :
1. A … is like a car. You see it on a farm.
4. Rock … is a sport.
7. A … is her parents' child.
9. … are animals. You often find them on farms.

Down ▼ :
2. A … is a bird. We eat their eggs.
3. … is a sport on water.
5. Our dog's … has our name on it.
6. A … is a man or woman with a farm.
8. A satnav has … .

Crossword answers:
1 ▶ TRACTOR
4 ▶ CLIMBING
7 ▶ DAUGHTER
9 ▶ SHEEP

What's the word?

1. Man kann Leute im Park <u>kennen lernen</u>. — You can <u>meet</u> people in the park.
2. <u>Mach dir</u> darüber keine <u>Sorgen</u>. — Don't <u>worry</u> about it.
3. Wir <u>kamen</u> am Sonntag <u>an</u>. — We <u>came</u> here on Sunday.
4. <u>Klicken</u> Sie hier, um einige Fotos zu sehen. — <u>Click</u> here to see some photos.
5. Man braucht die Schafe <u>nicht</u> zu füttern. Sie fressen Gras. — You <u>needn't</u> feed the sheep. They eat grass.
6. <u>Möchtest du</u> unseren Bauernhof sehen? — <u>Would you like</u> to see our farm?
7. <u>Ich möchte</u> Kanufahren. — <u>I'd like to</u> go canoeing.
8. <u>Ich möchte nicht</u> klettern gehen. — <u>I wouldn't like to</u> go rock climbing.
9. Ich <u>habe</u> die Hühner heute morgen <u>gefüttert</u>. — I <u>fed</u> the chickens this morning.

2 Put in the right words. Setze die richtigen Wörter ein.

> tractor · meets · came · like · farmer · canoeing · wouldn't · fed · needn't

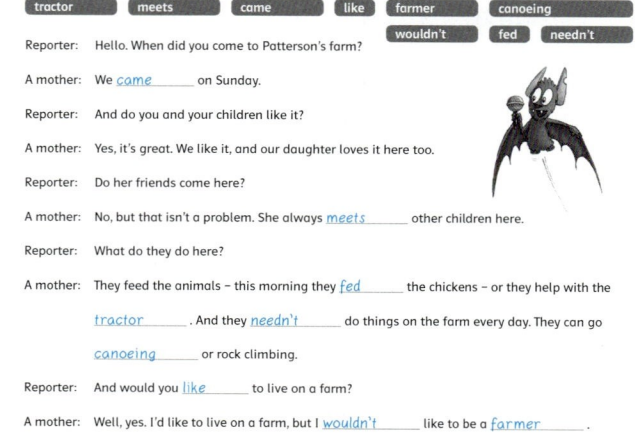

Reporter: Hello. When did you come to Patterson's farm?

A mother: We <u>came</u> on Sunday.

Reporter: And do you and your children like it?

A mother: Yes, it's great. We like it, and our daughter loves it here too.

Reporter: Do her friends come here?

A mother: No, but that isn't a problem. She always <u>meets</u> other children here.

Reporter: What do they do here?

A mother: They feed the animals – this morning they <u>fed</u> the chickens – or they help with the <u>tractor</u>. And they <u>needn't</u> do things on the farm every day. They can go <u>canoeing</u> or rock climbing.

Reporter: And would you <u>like</u> to live on a farm?

A mother: Well, yes. I'd like to live on a farm, but I <u>wouldn't</u> like to be a <u>farmer</u>. They always get up very early and work very late.

What's the word?

1. Ich mag das <u>Land</u>, aber ich mag auch Städte. — I like the <u>country</u>, but I like towns too.
2. Wir gehen oft auf <u>Klassenfahrten</u>. — We often go on <u>school trips</u>.
3. Im Sommer fahren wir immer in <u>Urlaub</u>. — We always go on <u>holiday</u> in the summer.
4. Meine Großmutter wohnt <u>auf dem Land</u>. — My grandmother lives <u>in the country</u>.
5. Unser Haus ist <u>in der Nähe</u> von einem Park. — Our house is <u>near</u> a park.
6. Unsere Schule ist sehr <u>modern</u>. — Our school is very <u>modern</u>.
7. Unsere Cousins treffen <u>uns</u> jeden Sommer. — Our cousins meet <u>us</u> every summer.
8. Dieses Spiel ist <u>langweilig</u>. — This game is <u>boring</u>.
9. Klettern kann <u>beängstigend</u> sein. — Rock climbing can be <u>scary</u>.

3 Read and put in the right words. Lies die Texte und füge das passende Adjektiv ein.

> scary · cold · awful · modern · beautiful · boring

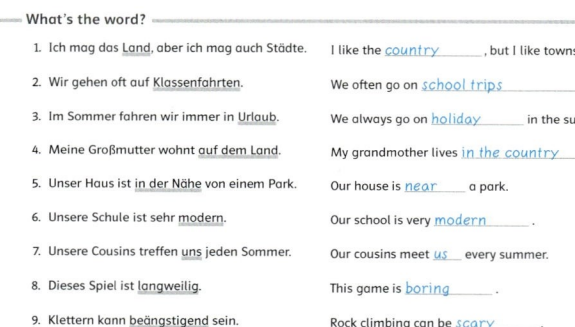

1. Our house is new and it has new technology in the kitchen and in the bathroom.
Our house is <u>modern</u>.

2. He does not like boys and girls, and he hates me too. He is not a nice man.
He's <u>awful</u>.

3. I like Alex's picture. He's very good at art. And look at the colours!
Yes, the picture is <u>beautiful</u>.

4. I can't read this book. It isn't funny and it isn't interesting.
The book is <u>boring</u>.

5. I like the film. It's very exciting but I can't watch it because I can't sleep after that.
The film is <u>scary</u>.

6. It's May. It isn't winter now but I need more clothes. And let's make a fire.
It's <u>cold</u>.

4 Match the sentence parts. Ordne die Satzteile zu.

1. I love rock
2. We live in
3. Year 7TM are on
4. I'd like
5. I wouldn't
6. The game is

a) like to live in a town.
b) to have a dog.
c) the country.
d) very boring.
e) a school trip.
f) climbing.

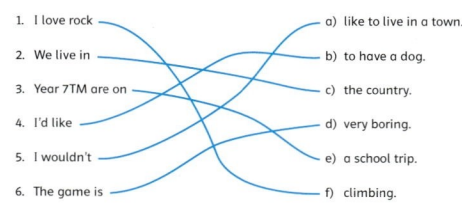

What's the word?

1. Ich habe eine blaue Jacke.
I have a blue _coat_ .

2. Wir können keine Jeans in der Schule tragen.
We can't wear _jeans_ at school.

3. Ich habe drei Schals, aber ich trage nur den Manchester United Schal.
I have three _scarves_ but I only wear the Manchester United _scarf_ .

4. Ich trage keine Schuhe im Haus.
I don't wear _shoes_ in the house.

5. Ich habe einen neuen Rock. Magst du ihn?
I have a new _skirt_ . Do you like it?

6. Wir können weiße oder blaue Socken in der Schule tragen.
We can wear white or blue _socks_ at school.

7. Ich liebe dein neues Sweatshirt.
I love your new _sweatshirt_ .

8. Ich trage Turnschuhe beim Tennis.
I wear _trainers_ for tennis.

9. Sie mag Äpfel.
She likes _apples_ .

10. Ich bin in einer neuen Klasse.
I'm in a new _class_ .

5 Write the words. Beschrifte die Kleidungsstücke auf Englisch.

1 _trainer_
2 _coat_
3 _jeans_
4 _scarf_
5 _sock_
6 _sweatshirt_
7 _shoe_
8 _skirt_

6 Answer the questions. Beantworte die Fragen.

1. It's cold. What do you wear? _coat, scarf, sweatshirt_

2. What do only girls wear? _skirt_

3. What do you wear with socks? _shoes, trainers_

What's the word?

1. Deine Hose ist schmutzig.
Your _trousers_ are dirty.

2. Im Sommer trage ich einen Rock und ein T-Shirt.
In summer I wear a skirt and a _T-shirt_ .

3. Kann ich dein Handy haben? Ich will ein Telefongespräch führen.
Can I have your mobile? I want to make a _phone call_ .

4. Wie geht's dir? – Mir geht's gut, danke.
How are you ? – I'm fine, thanks.

5. Ich habe lange Arme.
I have long _arms_ .

6. Mir war schlecht, aber es geht mir jetzt besser.
I was sick, but I'm _better_ now.

7. Mein Hobby ist Reiten.
My hobby is _horse riding_ .

8. Wir machen oft Picknicks im Sommer.
We often have _picnics_ in summer.

9. Und wir gehen Kanufahren. Dann tragen wir Helme.
And we go canoeing. Then we wear _helmets_ .

7 Look at the pictures and finish the sentences. Schau dir die Bilder an und vervollständige die Sätze.

1. She always wears a _helmet_ .
3. He loves _horse riding_ .
5. That's a cool _T-shirt_ .

2. She wants to make a _phone call_ .
4. Our dog likes _picnics_ .
6. We have two _chickens_ .

8 Write the words. Finde die Wörter und schreibe sie auf Englisch und Deutsch auf.

1. mars _arms – Arme_
2. kosc _sock – Socke_
3. retebt _better – besser_
4. urtosser _trousers – Hose_
5. methel _helmet – Helm_
6. cincpi _picnic – Picknick_

What's the word?

1. Was gibt's zum Abendessen?
What's for _dinner_ ?

2. Wales ist ein kleines Land.
Wales is a small country.

3. Es ist warm in der Küche.
It's _warm_ in the kitchen.

4. Hör damit auf!
Stop that!

5. Mein Bruder hat gestern mein Fahrrad kaputtgemacht. Er macht immer alles kaputt.
My brother _broke_ my bike yesterday. He always _breaks_ things.

6. Du musst einen Helm tragen.
You _must_ wear a helmet.

7. Du hast das T-Shirt gestern getragen.
You _wore_ that T-shirt yesterday.

9 Find six words.

a) Find the English verbs in the infinitive or simple past. (↓ and →) Finde die englischen Verben im Infinitiv oder in der Vergangenheitsform.

A	C	B	O	S	M	N	T
W	O	R	C	B	E	D	S
E	M	O	P	I	E	E	T
A	E	K	O	E	T	X	O
R	F	E	E	D	N	I	P

b) Put in the rights verbs from a). Setze das richtige Verb aus a) ein.

1. You must _feed_ your pet every day.
2. Can I _wear_ my new jeans?
3. Come and _meet_ my friends!
4. Yesterday I _broke_ my mobile.
5. Lots of people _come_ to our town in August.
6. That noise is awful! Please _stop_ !

What's the word?

1. Dein Bruder ist freundlich.
Your brother is _friendly_ .

2. Lass uns nächstes Jahr zurückkommen.
Let's come _back_ next year.

3. Wir haben morgen einen Test.
We have a _test_ tomorrow.

4. Du bist spät! – Es tut mir leid.
You are late! – _Sorry_ .

5. Gestern Nacht haben wir eine Nachtwanderung gemacht.
We went on a _night walk_ last night.

6. Du spielst gut Fußball, aber ich bin der Beste.
You're good at football but I'm _the best_ !

7. Geh:'s dir gut? – Ja, mir geht's gut.
Are you OK? – Yes, _I'm fine_ .

8. Bis bald!
See you soon !

10 Complete the words and write the sentences in German. Vervollständige die Wörter in den Sätzen mit den fehlenden Buchstaben. Übersetze die Sätze ins Deutsche.

A A A A A A E E E E E I I
O O O O O O O O O U U

1. S_ee_ y_o_u s_oo_n! — _Bis bald!_
2. L_e_t's g_o_ _o_n _a_ n_i_ght w_a_lk. — _Lass uns eine Nachtwanderung machen._
3. Th_a_t's my sw_e_atsh_i_rt. — _Das ist mein Sweatshirt._
4. Is th_a_t ph_o_ne c_a_ll f_o_r m_e_? — _Ist das Telefongespräch für mich?_
5. It's y_o_ur s_o_ck. — _Das ist deine Socke._

11 Match the questions and answers. Ordne die Fragen und Antworten richtig zu.

1. How are you?
2. You want to go?
3. Would you like to go canoeing?
4. Where do you live?
5. I love it here. Must we go home tomorrow?
6. Hey Do you have my helmet?

a) – Oh sorry! Here you are!
b) – I'm fine, thanks.
c) – In the country.
d) – Yes, but let's come back next year.
e) – Goodbye. See you soon!
f) – No thanks! That's scary.

What's the word?

1. Wie ist das Wetter heute? — *What's the weather like* today?
2. Heute ist es bewölkt und grau in Schottland. — It's *cloudy* and grey in Scotland today.
3. Das Meer ist oft kalt um England herum. — The sea is often *cold* around England.
4. Es ist immer heiß in Australien. — It's always *hot* in Australia.
5. Es regnet viel in Manchester. — It *rains* a lot in Manchester.
6. Es ist oft sonnig in London. — It's often *sunny* in London.
7. Es ist warm. Ich brauche meine Jacke nicht. — It's *warm*. I don't need my coat.
8. Deine Schuhe sind nass. — Your shoes are *wet*.
9. Es ist nicht kalt, aber es ist windig. — It's not cold but it's *windy*.

12 Look at the pictures and complete the sentences. Schau dir die Bilder an und vervollständige die Sätze.

1. It's *sunny*.
2. It's *windy*.
3. It's *cloudy*.
4. It's *wet.; rain*
5. It's *cold*.
6. It's *hot*.

13 Look at the map and complete the sentences. Schau dir die Karte und vervollständige die Sätze.

Yesterday the weather wasn't bad in Scotland.
It was very *cold*, but it was *sunny* too.
It wasn't so good in Manchester – it *rained* in
the morning and was *wet* all day. In Devon
the weather was better – it was *warm* but it
was *windy* too. In Birmingham it was *cloudy*
and grey. The best weather was in London – it was
sunny and *hot*.

What's the word?

1. Wir wollen um 11 Uhr eine Nachtwanderung machen. — We want to *go on a night walk* at 11 p.m.
2. Nachts ist es dunkel. — It's *dark* at night.
3. Ich habe ein komisches Geräusch gehört. — I *heard* a funny noise.
4. Es hat geregnet und ich wurde nass. — It rained and I *got* wet.
5. Es war gruselig, weil es dunkel war. — It was scary *because* it was dark.
6. Wir haben Fisch und Pommes zu Mittag gegessen. — We *ate* fish and chips for lunch.
7. Kannst du mich heute Abend anrufen? — Can you *phone* me this evening?
8. Bitte beantworte die Frage. — Please *answer* the question.
9. Der Urlaub war fantastisch. — The holiday was *fantastic*.

14 Put in the verbs in the past tense. Setze die Vergangenheitsformen der Verben ein.

`ask` `be` `be` `come` `go` `eat` `get` `hear` `see` `tell` `wear`

Last weekend my family and I *went* for a night walk. It was very cold, so we *wore* coats.
At first it was very exciting. But we walked for a long time, and I *got* very tired. I didn't want to walk
back to the farm. My brothers were tired too, but they are 15, and I am only 11. We *ate* chocolate, but
I was tired. I wanted to go by bus, but Dad *told* us he had no money. "Can't you help me, Dad?"
I asked. "I'm so tired."
Then we *heard* a funny noise. "What was that?" I *asked*. "I don't know," answered my dad.
We walked and walked, but we didn't talk. We all listened for the noise. Then we heard it. What was it?
A man? An animal? It *was* scary but I wasn't tired.
We walked fast, and 15 minutes later we *were* back at the farm.
I was the fastest and I was the first. Then I heard the noise and looked behind me. I *saw* my dad
with his mobile in his hand. The noise *came* from his mobile. "Dad!" I shouted, "It was you.
Why did you do that? That was not funny." Dad said, "Well, I only helped you! We're at the farm now."

What's the word?

1. Ich lese oft nachts mit einer Taschenlampe. — I often read at night with a *torch*.
2. Devon ist ein schöner Ort in England. — *Devon* is a beautiful place in England.
3. Spielst du gern Karten? — Do you like to play *cards*?
4. — That's my *alarm clock*.
5. Ich schreibe jeden Tag SMS. — I write *text messages* every day.
6. Wir schauen Basketball im Fernsehen. — We watch *basketball* on TV.
7. Man schreibt „Mit den besten Wünschen" am Ende von Postkarten. — You write "*Best wishes*" at the end of postcards.
8. Grüße meine Mutter und meinen Vater von mir. — *Say hi to* my mum and dad.
9. Ich hörte das Telefon rechtzeitig. — I heard the telephone *in time*.

15 Complete the crossword. Vervollständige das Kreuzworträtsel.

Across ▶:
1. It rained. Now I'm ....
3. People play ... in every country.
4. You can write a text ... on your mobile.
5. I was in ... for the bus – I wasn't late.
7. It was really, really great – it was ....
10. Our dog loves a night ... too.
11. I don't need an ... clock. I have my mobile.

Down ▼:
2. You write "Best ..." at the end of a postcard.
4. They play ... a lot in the USA.
6. It's always ... at night.
8. It's dark. I need a ....
9. It's not cold and it's not hot. – No, it's ....

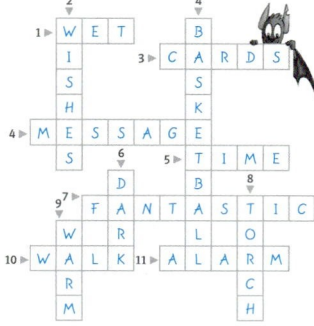

Crossword answers:
1 WET
3 CARDS
4 MESSAGE
5 TIME
7 FANTASTIC
10 WALK
11 ALARM

What's the word?

1. Gestern fiel ich in den Fluss. — Yesterday I *fell* into the *river*.
2. Es gibt ein Problem mit deinen Hausaufgaben. — There's a *problem* with your homework.
3. Er hat große Füße. — He has big *feet*.
4. Oh, mein Fuß. Er steckt fest. — Oh, my *foot*. It's *stuck*.
5. Ich kriege ihn nicht aus dem Matsch heraus. — I can't get it *out of* the *mud*.
6. Das Foto ist sehr dunkel. Ich sehe sein Gesicht nicht. — The photo is very dark. I can't see his *face*.
7. Ziehe nicht an meinem Schal! — Don't *pull* my scarf!
8. Ziehe nicht an der Tür. Du musst schieben. — Don't pull the door. You must *push*.
9. Ich sagte, „Nicht ziehen." — I *said*, "Don't pull."

16 The boy and his dog. Put in the right words and find another word. Trage die richtigen Wörter ein und finde das Lösungswort.

1. The boy has two ... and the dog has four. They walk on them.
2. The boy has two ... and his hands are at the end.
3. The boy has five ... on every hand.
4. The dog and the boy have a ....
5. The dog has a big ... and the boy has a small ....
6. The boy has two ... but the dog only has feet.

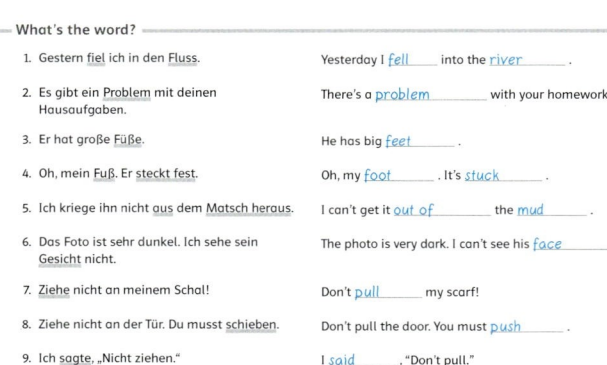

1 feet
2 arms
3 fingers
4 face
5 nose
6 hands

What's the word?
The boy's dog is also the boy's ... *friend*

17 Find the words and write them in the right table. Finde zehn Verben in der Vergangenheitsform und schreibe sie in die richtige Tabellenspalte.

1. ehudsp
2. eta
3. isda
4. tog
5. krebo
6. reow
7. ludelp
8. wanderse
9. rehad
10. petopds

regelmäßig	unregelmäßig
pushed	said
pulled	ate
answered	got
stopped	broke
	wore
	heard

What's the word?

1. Rachel sitzt in einem Rollstuhl, weil sie nicht laufen kann.

   Rachel sits in a <u>wheelchair</u> because she can't walk.

2. Lass uns schauen, was in der Schatzkiste ist.

   Let's see what's in the <u>cache box</u> .

3. Man benötigt GPS für Geocaching.

   You need GPS for <u>geocaching</u> .

4. Es gab keinen Schatz in der Schatzkiste.

   There was no <u>cache</u> in the cache box.

5. Es ist heute wirklich sonnig. Du musst eine Mütze tragen.

   It's really sunny today. You must wear a <u>cap</u> .

6. Nur Mädchen tragen Blusen.

   Only girls wear <u>blouses</u> .

7. T-Shirts und Blusen sind Tops.

   T-shirts and blouses are <u>tops</u> .

8. Bei heißem Wetter trage ich immer eine kurze Hose.

   I always wear <u>shorts</u> in hot weather.

18 Look at the pictures and write the words. Schau dir die Bilder an und schreibe die Wörter auf.

<u>blouse</u>   <u>shorts</u>   <u>cap</u>   <u>wheelchair</u>

<u>cache box</u>   <u>mud</u>   <u>torch</u>   <u>card</u>

19 Find the words. Write the English and German words.
Finde die Wörter. Schreibe sie auf Englisch und Deutsch auf.

shortsblousewheelchaircapgeocachingtop

<u>shorts – Shorts; kurze Hose</u>   <u>cap – Kappe; Mütze</u>

<u>blouse – Bluse</u>   <u>geocaching – Geocaching</u>

<u>wheelchair – Rollstuhl</u>   <u>top – Top</u>

What's the word?

1. Das Bild ist sehr bunt.

   That picture is very <u>colourful</u> .

2. Sie ist ein sehr hübsches Mädchen.

   She's a very <u>pretty</u> girl.

3. Es ist neblig. Ich kann nicht viel sehen.

   It's <u>foggy</u> . I can't see very much.

4. Das Wetter ist mild in England. Es ist nicht sehr heiß oder kalt.

   The weather is <u>mild</u> in England. It isn't very hot or cold.

5. Meine Schuhe waren nass, aber sie sind jetzt trocken.

   My shoes were wet, but they are <u>dry</u> now.

6. ⟷ warm

   It's <u>cool</u> today.

7. Seine Kleidung ist immer sehr schick.

   His clothes are always very <u>chic</u> .

8. John sitzt hinter mir in der Klasse.

   John sits <u>behind</u> me in class.

9. Er ist zehn Minuten zu spät.

   He's ten <u>minutes</u> late.

20 Write the opposites. Schreibe die Gegenteile auf.

1. into – <u>out of</u>

2. wet – <u>dry</u>

3. warm – <u>cool</u>

4. grey – <u>colourful</u>

5. hot – <u>cold</u>

6. exciting – <u>boring</u>

7. cloudy – <u>sunny</u>

8. warm – <u>cool</u>

9. left – <u>right</u>

21 Put a circle around the odd one out. Write it in German. Welches Wort passt nicht in die Reihe? Kreise es ein. Schreibe es auf Deutsch auf.

1. cool • mild • (weather) • warm   <u>Wetter</u>

2. (awful) • beautiful • chic • pretty   <u>furchtbar; schrecklich</u>

3. foggy • (friendly) • sunny • windy   <u>freundlich</u>

4. (back) • behind • opposite • under   <u>zurück</u>

5. face • (minute) • finger • foot   <u>Minute</u>

What's the word?

1. Komm jetzt! Wir sind spät.

   <u>Come on</u> ! We're late.

2. Schau das Pferd an! Seine Nase ist blau.

   Look at that horse! <u>Its</u> nose is blue.

3. Das Schaf steckt im Schlamm fest.

   The sheep <u>is stuck in the mud</u> .

4. Das ist super! Gut gemacht!

   That's great! <u>Well done</u> !

5. Was können wir jetzt machen? Irgendeine Idee?

   What can we do now? <u>Any idea</u> ?

6. Wo ist mein Handy? – Lass uns danach suchen.

   Where's my mobile? – Let's <u>look for</u> it.

22 Match the words.

a) Match the word parts and write them in German. Ordne die Teile der Wörter richtig zu und schreibe sie auf Deutsch auf.

get	time
come	lost
free	up
get	on
in	of
look	and about
look	time
out	at
out	for

<u>get up – aufstehen</u>

<u>Come on! – Komm jetzt!</u>

<u>free time – Freizeit</u>

<u>get lost – sich verirren</u>

<u>in time – rechtzeitig</u>

<u>look for – suchen (nach)</u>

<u>look at – anschauen</u>

<u>out and about – unterwegs</u>

<u>out of – aus ... heraus</u>

b) Put the words from a) in the sentences. Setzte die Wörter aus a) in die Sätze ein.

1. Oh, no! It's five o'clock. <u>Come on</u> ! We're late.

2. I can't find my coat. Can you <u>look for</u> it in your house, please?

3. <u>Look at</u> that horse! Isn't it beautiful?

4. Get <u>out of</u> the sea! There's a shark.

5. Are we <u>in time</u> for the bus? – Yes, its only quarter to four.

6. What do you do in your <u>free time</u> ? – Oh, I play basketball.

7. I never see my brother at the weekend. He's always <u>out and about</u> .

8. <u>Get up</u> ! It's eight thirty, and you're in bed.

9. With GPS on my phone I never <u>get lost</u> .

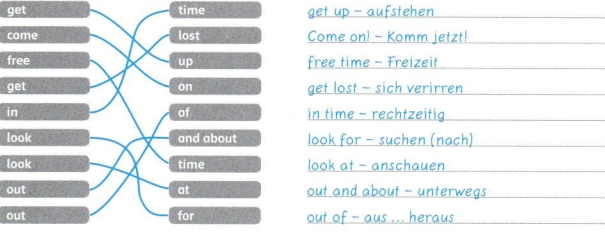

Goodbye

Bestandteil von
ISBN 978-3-12-**548801**-4

What's the word?

1. Das ist mein Schlafzimmer.

This is my _____ .

2. Ich habe einen  .

I have a _____ .

3. Das ist ein schönes Poster.

This is a nice _____ .

4. Der Fußball ist auf dem Bett.

The football is _____ the _____ .

5. Ich habe einen .

I have a _____ .

6. Das ist eine Kiste.

This is a _____ .

7. Das Buch ist auf dem Regal.

The _____ is on the _____ .

8. Mein Handy ist schwarz.

My _____ is black.

9. Lukes T-Shirt ist blau.

Luke's _____ is blue.

8 Write the words. Finde die Wörter und schreibe sie auf.

1. beoomrd _____

2. potsre _____

3. xbo _____

4. cairh _____

5. kobo _____

6. tlabe _____

7. miloeb heonp _____

8. T-ritsh _____

9. shesvel _____

10. deb _____

9 Look at the picture and write the words. Schau dir das Bild an und schreibe die Wörter auf.

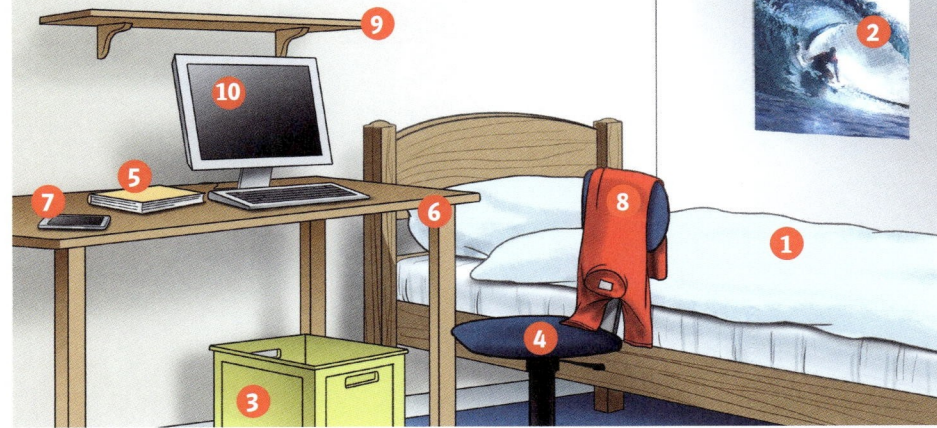

1 _____
2 _____
3 _____
4 _____
5 _____
6 _____
7 _____
8 _____
9 _____
10 _____

What's the word?

1. Es ist Samstag.   It's _____ .

2. Ich bin zu Hause.   I'm _____ .

3. Wer ist das?   _____ is it?

4. Ich bin es!   _____ !

5. Bist du bereit?   _____ ?

6. Ich kann meinen Fußball nicht finden.   _____ my football.

7. Er ist unter dem Bett.   It's _____ the bed.

8. Wir sind zu spät.   We're _____ .

10   Write the words in English and German.   Schreibe die Wörter auf Englisch und Deutsch auf.

1. er _____

2. es _____

3. wir _____

4. ihr _____

5. they _____

6. she _____

7. you _____

8. I _____

11   Put in the right words.   Setze die richtigen Wörter ein.

 late   at   It's   find   you   under   Who

1. I'm _____ home.

2. I can't _____ my football.

3. My dog is _____ the table.

4. _____ is it?

5. We're _____ .

6. Are _____ ready?

7. _____ Saturday.

What's the word?

1. Ich habe ein neues Handy.

   I have a _____ mobile.

2. Welche Farbe hat dein Handy?

   _____ your mobile?

3. Es ist in meinem Zimmer.

   It's in my _____ .

4. Dein Regal ist ein Durcheinander.

   Your shelf is a _____ .

5. Wo ist mein Fußball?

   _____ is my football?

6. Der Fußball ist in deiner Box.

   The football is in _____ box.

7. Nein, das ist falsch!

   _____ , that's _____ !

8. Das ist richtig!

   That's _____ !

9. Was ist das?

   _____ that?

10. Da sind Fledermäuse.

    _____ bats.

11. Da ist mein Fahrrad.

    _____ my bike.

12 Put in the right words. Setze die richtigen Wörter ein.

Sally

"This is my _____ mobile."

"_____ is your mobile?"

"What _____ is your T-shirt?"

"Your room is a _____ !"

"_____ that? A poster?"

"_____ are cats on your poster."

Janet

"Cool!"

"It's in my _____ ."

"It's green."

"No, no! That's _____ !"

"Yes, that's _____ ."

"Yes, and _____ a dog too."

wrong
There
right
colour
new
room
Where
mess
there's
What's

13 Complete the words. Vervollständige die Wörter mit den fehlenden Buchstaben.

A   A   A   E   E   E   E   E   E   E   E   E   I   O   O   O

O   O   O

O   U

1. r___m

2. wr__ng

3. wh__

4. r_ght

5. f___tb_ll

6. n_w

7. m__ss

8. wh_r_

9. y__r

10. wh_t's

11. th_r_ __r_

12. th_r_'s

What's the word?

1. In unserem Garten gibt es einen <u>Baum</u>.

   There's a _____ in our garden.

2. Meine Mutter ist im <u>Haus</u>.

   My mother is in the _____ .

3. Sie ist <u>beschäftigt</u>.

   She is _____ .

4. <u>Später</u> spiele ich Fußball.

   _____ I play football.

5. Ich habe einen <u>merkwürdigen</u> <u>Traum</u>.

   I have a _____ .

7. [image: moon and stars]

   _____

8. <u>Niemand</u> ist hier, und es gibt kein <u>Geräusch</u>.

   _____ is here, and there's no _____ .

9. <u>Dann</u> spielen wir Fußball.

   _____ we play football.

10. [image: ladder]

    _____

11. [image: puff of wind]

    _____

14 Find ten words.

a) Find the English words. (↓ and →) Finde die englischen Wörter.

B	D	N	T	H	O	U	S	E	G
U	R	I	G	H	T	T	H	E	N
S	V	G	G	H	L	R	B	C	V
Y	B	H	Y	D	R	E	A	M	K
L	A	T	E	R	G	E	H	J	A
G	N	O	O	N	E	D	S	B	S
A	P	I	F	U	N	N	Y	J	D

b) Write the words. Schreibe die Wörter auf.

1. richtig _____

2. später _____

3. beschäftigt _____

4. Haus _____

5. niemand _____

6. Nacht _____

7. Baum _____

8. Traum _____

9. merkwürdig _____

10. danach _____

15 Write the words. Finde die Wörter und schreibe sie auf.

1. dadrel _____

2. usohe _____

3. diwn _____

4. ysbu _____

What's the word?

1. zu Hause

_____

2. Ich kann meine Katze nicht finden.
   Na ja, schau mal im Garten nach.

   I can't find my cat.

   _____ in the garden.

3. Danke.

   _____ .

4. Meine Mutter ist in der Küche.

   My mother is in the _____ .

5. Mein Vater ist im Badezimmer.

   My father is in the _____ .

6. Mein Bruder ist im Wohnzimmer.

   My brother is in the _____ .

7. Mein Hund Sherlock ist im Schlafzimmer.

   My dog Sherlock is in the _____ .

16 **Look at the picture and write the words.** Schau dir das Bild an und schreibe die Wörter auf.

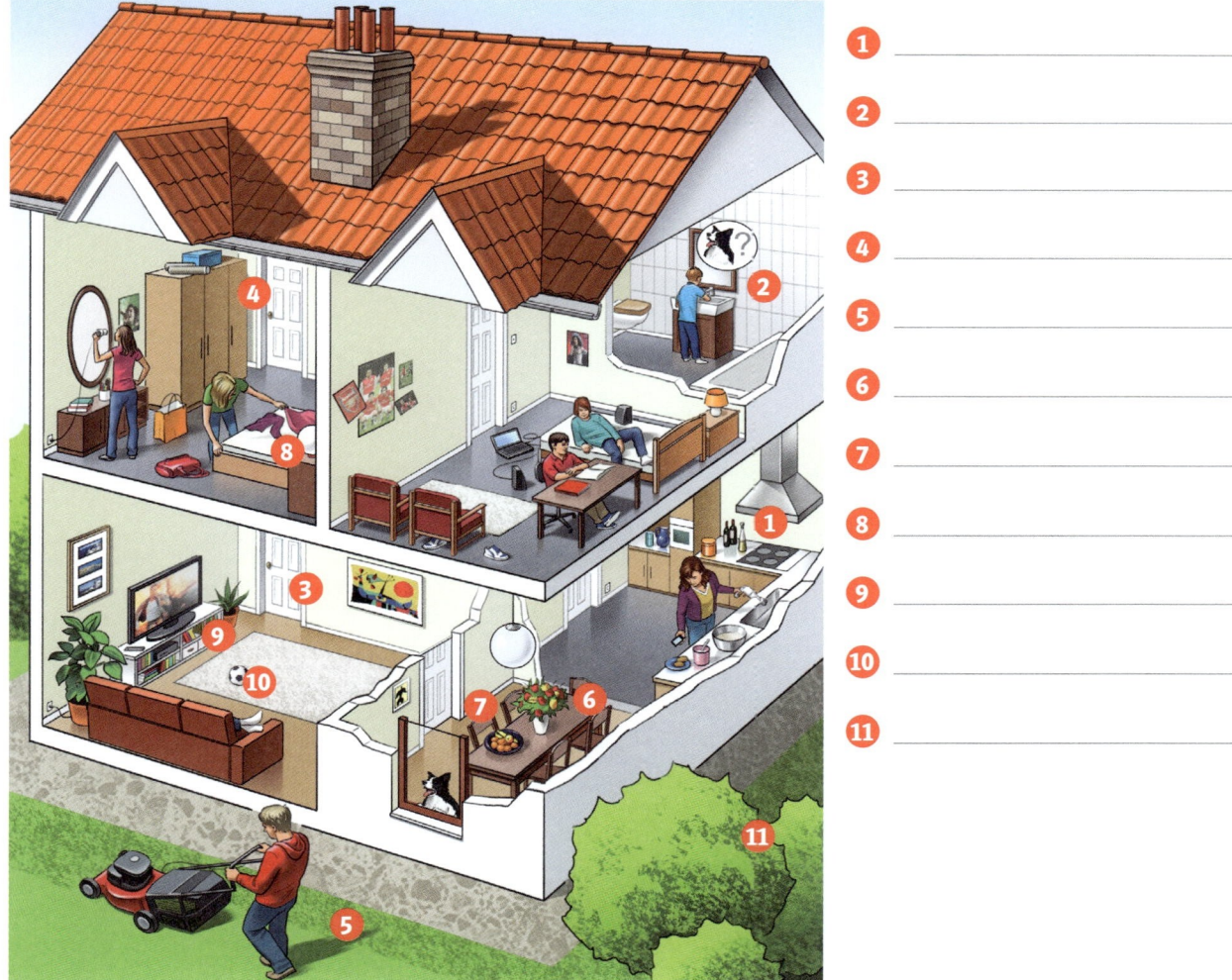

1 _____

2 _____

3 _____

4 _____

5 _____

6 _____

7 _____

8 _____

9 _____

10 _____

11 _____

What's the word?

1. Ich bin im Esszimmer.   I'm in the _____ .

2. Lasst uns Tennis spielen.   _____ tennis.

3. Ich mag das Spiel.   I like the _____ .

4. Es ist großartig.   It's _____ .

5. Schau mal! Da ist mein Hund.   _____ ! There's my dog.

6. Er ist ein witziger Hund.   He's a _____ dog.

17 **Write the words.** Finde die Wörter und schreibe sie auf Englisch und Deutsch auf.

1. ufynn _____

2. kool _____

3. htkans _____

4. mdrae _____

5. mega _____

6. nidign orom _____

7. etl's apyl _____

8. egatr _____

18 **Put in the right words.** Setze die richtigen Wörter ein.

| dining room | game | Let's play | Look | funny |

1. Let's play a computer _____ .

2. Ben the bat is _____ .

3. The table is in the _____ .

4. _____ , this is our house.

5. _____ football in the garden.

What's the word?

1. Ich mag meine Eltern.

   I like my _____ .

2. Mein Onkel und meine Tante sind lustig.

   My _____ and my _____ are funny.

3. Ich habe einen Cousin.

   I have a _____ .

4. Meine Großmutter ist cool.

   My _____ is cool.

5. Mein Großvater kommt aus Greenwich.

   My _____ is from Greenwich.

19 Right or wrong?

a) Look at page 194. Are the sentences right or wrong? Tick ✔ the right box.
   Schaue dir Seite 194 im Buch an. Sind die Sätze richtig oder falsch? Kreuze ✔ an.

	right	wrong
1. Henry is Adam's grandfather.	☐	☐
2. Lisa is Adam's mum.	☐	☐
3. Sarah is Adam's brother.	☐	☐
4. Isabel is Adam's sister.	☐	☐
5. Matthew and Lucy are Helen and Kevin's parents.	☐	☐
6. Henry and Anne are Adam's grandparents.	☐	☐
7. Anne is Lucy's grandmother.	☐	☐

b) Complete the sentences. Vervollständige die Sätze.

1. _____ and _____ are Adam's cousins.

2. _____ is Adam's aunt.

3. _____ and _____ are Adam's parents.

4. Daniel is Adam's _____ .

5. Isabel is an only child. She has no _____ .

6. Lucy is Adam's _____ and Matthew is Adam's _____ .

20 Complete the words. Vervollständige die Wörter mit den fehlenden Buchstaben.

A A A A A E E E E I O O U U U

1. p _ r _ nts

2. _ ncl _

3. gr _ ndm _ th _ r

4. c _ _ _ s _ n

5. _ _ nt

6. gr _ ndf _ th _ r

What's the word?

1. Der Turnschuh ist im Kleiderschrank.

The _____ is in the _____ .

2. Dein Schal auch.

Your _____ too.

3. Ich mag deinen Teppich.

I like your _____ .

4.

_____

5. Da ist ein Geräusch. Es ist der Wecker.

There's a noise. It's the _____ .

6.

_____

7. Das Baumhaus ist fertig.

The _____ is _____ .

8.

_____

21 Complete the crossword. Vervollständige das Kreuzworträtsel.

Across ▶ :

1.

3. English word for 'fertig'

5. English word for 'Lampe'

8.

10. … is from trees.

11. One scarf, two …

Down ▼ :

2.

4.

6. Your mother and your father = your …

7. A house in a tree is a … .

9.

12. There's a … in the tree house. Is it a bat?

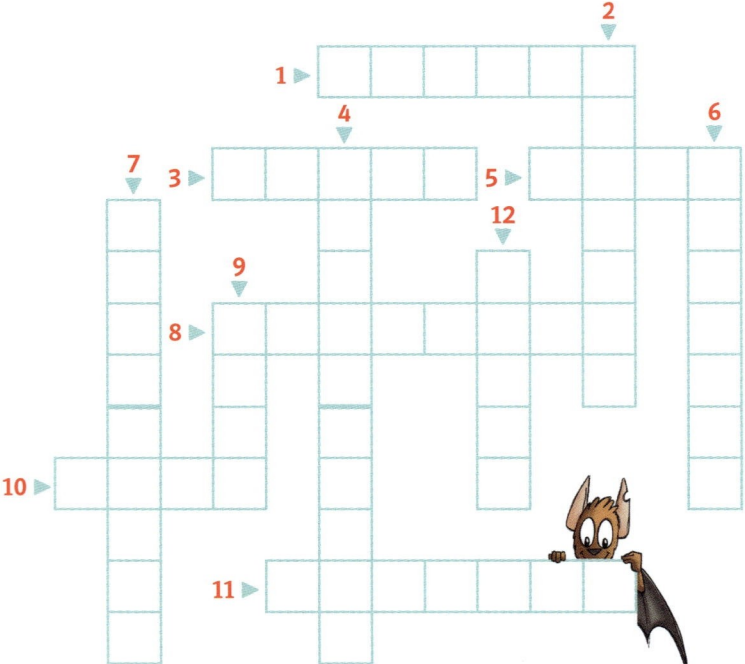

What's the word?

1. Meine Schule ist toll.

   My _____ is great.

2. Ich gehe auf die Thomas Tallis Schule.

   I _____ Thomas Tallis School.

3. Ich mag diesen Ort.

   I like this _____ .

4. Ich bin in der 5. Klasse.

   I'm in _____ 7.

5. In Deutschland haben wir keine Uniformen in der Schule.

   In Germany we have no _____

   _____ .

6. Ich mag unsere Cafeteria in der Schule.

   I like our _____ at school.

7. Hunde sind meine Lieblingstiere.

   Dogs are my _____ animals.

1 About me. Stelle dich auf Englisch vor.

1. Hallo, ich heiße … . _____

2. Ich bin … Jahre alt. _____

3. Ich komme aus … . _____

4. Ich gehe auf die … Schule. _____

5. Ich bin in der fünften Klasse. _____

6. Mein Lieblingstier ist … . _____

2 Look at the pictures and write the words. Schau dir die Bilder an und schreibe die Wörter auf.

This is my new _____ .

I _____ to a cool school.

I'm in _____ 7.

This is me in my _____ .

It's OK. Blue is my _____ colour.

This is the _____ .

It's my favourite _____ at Thomas Tallis.

What's the word?

1. Wir haben einen tollen Pausenhof an unserer Schule.

   We have a great _____ at our school.

2. Ich kann in der Cafeteria essen.

   I can _____ in the cafeteria.

3. Ich mag das Essen dort.

   I like the _____ there.

4. Mein Klassenzimmer ist neben dem Park.

   My _____ is next to the park.

5. Herr Swindon ist unser Klassenlehrer.

   _____ Swindon is our _____ .

6. Er ist sehr nett.

   He's _____ nice.

7. Unser Englischlehrer ist auch nett.

   Our _____ is nice too.

8. Ich mag Mathe.

   I like _____ .

3 Complete the words. Vervollständige die Wörter mit den fehlenden Buchstaben.

1. Mr Smith is our English t___ch__r.

2. My cl__ssr___m is my f__v___r__t__ pl__c__.

3. I like our t__t__r.

4. We play football in the pl__ygr___nd.

5. We ___t in the c__f__t__r___.

6. I like my new friends __t sch___l.

A	A	A	A	A	A
A	A	A	E	E	E
E	E	E	E	I	I
O	O	O	O	O	O
O	U	U	U		

4 Right or wrong? Richtig oder falsch?
Look at pages 32/33. Are the sentences right or wrong? Tick ✔ the right box. Correct the wrong words.
Schau die die Seiten 32/33 im Buch an. Sind die Sätze richtig oder falsch? Kreuze ✔ an.
Korrigiere die Wörter, die falsch sind.

	right	wrong	correction
1. The name of Holly's school is Thomas Tailor School.	☐	☐	_____
2. Holly's school uniform is black and green.	☐	☐	_____
3. Mr Swindon is her English teacher and her tutor.	☐	☐	_____
4. Holly's favourite place is the playground.	☐	☐	_____
5. She's in tutor group 7RS.	☐	☐	_____

What's the word?

1. Ich spreche gern mit meinem Freund Luke.

   I like to _____ my friend Luke.

2. Frau Warren ist die Hausmeisterin an unserer Schule.

   _____ Warren is the _____ at our school.

3. Ich singe gerne.

   I like to _____ .

4. Ich gehe mit meinen Freunden ins Tonstudio.

   I go to the _____ with my friends.

5. Ich mag Fußball nicht.

   _____ football.

6. Es sind 28 Schüler in unserer Klasse.

   There are 28 _____ in our _____ .

---

5 **Look at the pictures and write the verbs.** Schau dir die Bilder an und schreibe die Verben auf.

_____ _____ _____ _____

---

6 **Find the words.** Knacke den Code und finde die Wörter. Zu jeder Zahl gehört ein Buchstabe.

1. __ __ __ __
   11 5 8 6

2. __ __ __ __ __   __ __ __ __ __
   13 15 13 4 9   6 9 4 15 12

3. __ __ __ __ __ __ __
   11 13 15 3 2 8 13

4. __ __ __ __ __ __ __ __ __
   14 7 9 2 13 7 10 2 9

5. __ __ __ __ __ __ __ __ __   __ __ __ __ __ __
   9 2 14 4 9 3 5 8 6   11 13 15 3 5 4

6. __ __ __ __
   13 7 1 10

A	C	D	E	G	I	K	L
7	14	3	2	6	5	10	1

N	O	P	R	S	T	U
8	4	12	9	11	13	15

What's the word?

1. Ich kaufe ein Lineal für Mathe.

   I buy a _____ for Maths.

2. Ich kaufe einen Füller, einen Buntstift und einen Radiergummi für die Schule.

   I buy a _____ , a _____ and an _____ for school.

3. Ich mag meine Tasche.

   I like my _____ .

4. Für Englisch haben wir zwei Übungshefte.

   We have two _____ for English.

7 Look at the pictures and write the words in English and German. Schau dir die Bilder an und schreibe die Wörter auf Englisch und Deutsch.

_____

_____

_____

_____

_____

_____

_____

8 Put in the right words. Setze die richtigen Wörter ein.

exercise books	cafeteria	school	students	pencils
classrooms	food	favourite	Maths	ruler
teacher	recording studio	bag		

At _____

There are 430 _____ and 20 _____ in our school.

We have a _____ and a _____ . The _____ is great.

My _____ teacher is Mr Swandon. He is my Maths _____ .

For _____ we buy a _____ and _____ . All my things are in my

new _____ – the _____ too.

What's the word?

1. Ich sitze neben dem Fenster.

I _____ next to the _____ .

2. Sprich bitte nicht mit ihr.

_____ to her, please.

3. Bitte singe nicht.

Don't sing, _____ .

4. Mein Name ist David. Nenn mich Dave.

My name is David. _____ Dave.

5. Dave ist ein guter Sänger.

Dave is a _____ .

6. Er kann auch tanzen.

He can _____ too.

7. Macht bitte eure Übungshefte zu.

_____ your exercise books, please.

9 **Look at the pictures and complete the sentences.** Schau dir die Bilder an und vervollständige die Sätze.

1. Don't _____ to your friends, please.

2. Don't _____ the window, please.

3. Don't _____ on the chair, please.

4. Don't _____ in the classroom, please.

5. Don't _____ now, please.

10 **Find the words. Write the English and German words.**
Finde die Wörter. Schreibe sie auf Englisch und Deutsch auf.

windowsitsingerpleasepencilexercisebookcallmegood

_____   _____

_____   _____

_____   _____

_____   _____

What's the word?

1. Ich mag Fußball wirklich.

   I _____ like football.

2. Es ist für dich.

   It's _____ you.

3. boy ⟷

   _____

4. Rede jetzt bitte nicht.

   Don't talk _____ , please.

5. Setz dich neben mich.

   _____ next to me.

6. Schau dir Luke an. Er hat ein grünes Fahrrad.

   _____ Luke. He has a green bike.

7. Der Talentwettbewerb ist nächste Woche.

   The _____ is _____ .

8. Schlagt bitte eure Bücher auf.

   _____ your books, please.

9. Und nehmt eure Übungshefte heraus.

   And _____ your exercise books.

11 My Wednesday at school.
Put in the verbs and put the sentences in the correct order.
Setze die Verben ein und bringe die Sätze in die richtige Reihenfolge.

| sit down | go ✓ | play | talk | open | take out | look at |

I _go___ to school. ☐ 1

I don't _____ and I _____ my teacher Mr Swindon. ☐

I _____ next to my friend and I _____ my bag. ☐

I go home and _____ football in the garden. ☐

I _____ my exercise book and my pen. Mr Swindon is here now. ☐

12 Write the words. Finde die Wörter und schreibe sie auf Englisch und Deutsch auf.

1. aket uot _____

2. latent wsoh _____

3. sti wond _____

4. lleyra _____

5. lgir _____

What's the word?

1. Schaut bitte an die Tafel.

    Please look at the _____ .

2. Bitte meldet euch.

    _____ , please.

3. Ich kann Nummer 1, 2 und 5 machen.

    I can _____ number 1, 2 and 5.

4. Ich kann Aufgabe 1 in mein Übungsheft schreiben.

    I can _____ exercise 1 in my exercise book.

5. Es sind drei Schüler in der Gruppe.

    There are three students in the _____ .

6. Es gibt eine Show in Greewich.

    There is a _____ in Greenwich.

7. Wo ist mein Buch? – Bitte schön.

    Where is my book? – _____ .

8. Danke, Luke.

    _____ , Luke.

9. Kaufe ein Übungsheft!

    Buy _____ exercise book!

13 Match the sentence parts. Ordne die Satzteile zu.

1. Holly is in	a) at the board, please.
2. Write	b) your hands up, please.
3. Look	c) number five?
4. Who can do	d) you, Mr Swindon.
5. Put	e) my group.
6. Thank	f) your name, please.

14 Look at the pictures and write the words in English and German. Schau dir die Bilder an und schreibe die Wörter auf Englisch und Deutsch auf.

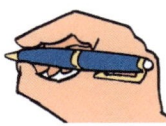   

_____ _____ _____ _____

What's the word?

1. Ich habe zehn Finger.

I have ten _____ .

2. Aber nur zwei Hände.

But only two _____ .

3. Ich höre gerne Musik.

I like to _____ music.

4. Aber ich habe kein Lieblingslied.

But I don't have a favourite _____ .

5. Lies bitte die Frage.

_____ the _____ , please.

6. Dann sag bitte die Antwort.

Then _____ the _____ , please.

7. Legt bitte die Stifte auf den Tisch.

_____ the pens on the table, please.

15 Find ten words.

a) Find the English words. (↓ and →) Finde die englischen Wörter.

S	G	A	F	F	H	A	N	D	S
F	W	N	Y	I	Y	F	Q	H	A
S	R	S	H	N	D	L	U	I	Y
O	I	W	F	G	F	R	E	A	D
N	T	E	L	E	L	Z	S	H	A
G	E	R	X	R	P	U	T	F	I
F	T	Z	P	S	L	G	I	P	L
L	I	S	T	E	N	R	O	O	O
Z	F	C	R	D	W	S	N	U	P

b) Write the words. Schreibe die Wörter auf.

_____

_____

16 Look at the pictures and write the words in English and German. Schau dir die Bilder an und schreibe die Wörter auf Englisch und Deutsch auf.

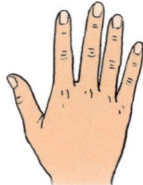 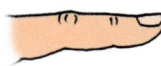  

_____ _____ _____ _____

What's the word?

1. Schau, das ist mein Stundenplan.

   Look, this is my _____ .

2.

   _____

3. Am Montag haben wir Englisch.

   On _____ we have _____ .

4. Mein Lieblingsfach ist Musik.

   My favourite _____ is _____ .

5. Am Dienstag haben wir Sportunterricht.

   On _____ we have _____ .

6. Wir haben Herrn Swindon in Mathe.

   We have Mr Swindon for _____ .

7. Frau Maier ist unsere Deutschlehrerin.

   Mrs Maier is our _____ teacher.

8. Am Mittwoch haben wir Französisch.

   On _____ we have _____ .

9. Am Donnerstag haben wir Technik.

   On _____ we have _____
   _____ .

10. Am Freitag haben wir Naturwissenschaft und Kunst.

    On _____ we have _____
    and _____ .

11. Am Samstag und Sonntag haben wir keine Schule.

    On _____ and _____
    we have no school.

17 Write the days of the week.

a) Write the days. Schreibe die Tage auf.

1. _ _ _ _ _ _ _ d a y   3. _ _ a _ _ _ d a y   5. _ r _ d a y   7. _ _ _ _ d a y

2. _ o _ d a y   4. _ _ _ d a y   6. _ h _ _ _ d a y

b) Write the days in the right order. Schreibe die Tage in der richtigen Reihenfolge auf.

M _____

_____

18 Put a circle around the odd one out. Welches Wort passt nicht in die Reihe? Kreise es ein.

1. Monday • Friday • Tuesday • days • Saturday

2. Art • Music • Design Technology • Science • classroom

3. classroom • cafeteria • playground • board

4. French • English • Maths • German

What's the word?

1. In der Pause gehe ich auf den Pausenhof.
   _____ I go to the playground.

2. Sportunterricht ist meine nächste Schulstunde. Und deine?
   PE is my next _____. And _____?

3. Französisch ist einfach.
   French is _____ .

4. Es ist wie Deutsch.
   It's _____ German.

5. Du hast Recht.
   _____ .

6. Ich bin auch gut in Französisch.
   _____ French too.

7. Das ist kein Witz.
   That's _____ a _____ .

8. Kannst du Rechtschreibung buchstabieren?
   Can you _____ ?

9. Nein, aber ich kann 'Alphabet' buchstabieren.
   No, but I can spell _____ .

10. Ich mag Kunst; es ist interessant.
    I like Art; it's _____ .

11. Am Dienstag haben wir Kunst.
    _____ we have Art.

12. Frau Kapoor macht die Überprüfung der Anwesenheit.
    _____ is with _____ Kapoor.

---

19 **Complete the words.** Vervollständige die Wörter mit den fehlenden Buchstaben.

1. sp_ll_ng

2. r_g_str_t_on

3. l_ss_n

4. _lph_b_t

5. _nt_r_st_ng

6. t_m_t_bl_

7. s_bj_ct

8. j_k_

---

20 **Choose the right answer.** Kreuze die für dich zutreffenden Aussagen an.

1. I'm good at ...   English ☐   Music ☐   Maths ☐   Art ☐   _____ ☐ .

2. Science ☐   Design Technology ☐   _____ ☐   ... is/are interesting.

3. I don't like _____ .

4. My timetable is ...   great ☐   good ☐   not good ☐ .

What's the word?

1. Das Mittagessen zu Hause ist gut.

   _____ at home is good.

2. Mein Onkel ist aus England.

   My _____ is from England.

3. Ich sehe ihn zu Hause.

   I _____ him at home.

4. Lass uns einen Streich spielen.

   Let's play a _____ .

5. Wir alle mögen Filme und Musik.

   We _____ like _____ and music.

6.

   _____

7.

   _____

8. Ich kann Freundschaften mit den Schülern aus meiner Klasse schließen.

   I can _____ the students in my tutor group.

9. Ich mag Kaugummi.

   I like _____ .

10.

    _____

---

21 Match the words. Ordne die Wörter richtig zu.

1. see	a)	Monday
2. week	b)	talk
3. uncle	c)	look
4. say	d)	family
5. trick	e)	food
6. saxophone	f)	T-shirt
7. jeans	g)	fun / funny
8. lunch	h)	music

22 Put a circle around the odd one out. Welches Wort passt nicht in die Reihe? Kreise es ein.

1. one • three • all • seven
2. bat • cat • guinea pig • girl
3. jeans • ruler • pen • eraser
4. Maths • English • lunch • Science
5. playground • classroom • cafeteria • bedroom

6. sing • talk • say • see
7. Mondcy • film • Tuesday • Friday
8. chewing gum • good • interesting • funny
9. caretaker • uncle • student • teacher
10. lesson • subject • dog • timetable

What's the word?

1. Ich kaufe einen <u>Taschenrechner</u> für Mathe.

   I buy a _____ for Maths.

2. In meinem <u>Federmäppchen</u> ist ein <u>Filzstift</u> und ein <u>Anspitzer</u>.

   In my _____ there is a _____ and a _____ .

3. Ich kaufe <u>Klebstoff</u> für den <u>Religionsunterricht</u>.

   I buy _____ for _____ .

4. Mein Lieblingsfach ist <u>Informationstechnik</u>.

   My favourite subject is _____ .

5. <u>Geschichte</u> und <u>Biologie</u> mag ich auch.

   I like _____ and _____ too.

6. <u>Erdkunde</u> ist <u>langweilig</u>.

   _____ is _____ .

7. <u>Französisch</u> ist <u>schwierig</u>.

   French is _____ .

23 Complete the crossword. Vervollständige das Kreuzworträtsel.

Across ▶ :

5.

8. Short form: Information Technology

10. English word for 'Biologie'

Down ▼ :

1.

3. Short form: Religious Education

4.

7. English word for 'Geschichte'

2.

6.

9. interesting ⟷

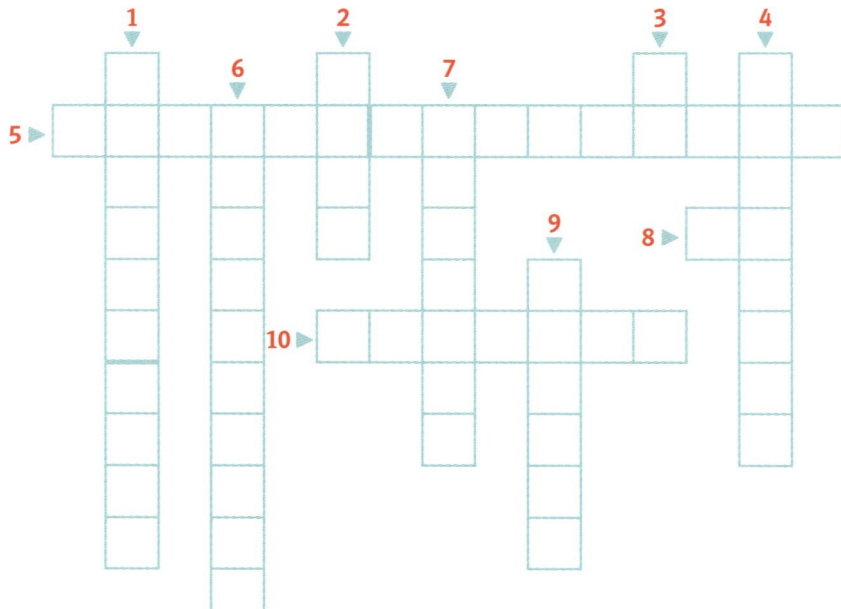

What's the word?

1. Wir haben Spaß.

   We have _____ .

2. Was ist dein Talent?

   What's your _____ ?

3. Gut gemacht!

   _____ !

4. Michael Jackson ist ein Star.

   Michael Jackson is a _____ .

5. Ich mag indisches Essen.

   I like _____ food.

6. Lass uns in ein Restaurant gehen.

   Let's go to a _____ .

24 Find ten words.

a) Find the English words. (↓ and →) Finde die englischen Wörter.

F	H	T	R	I	C	K	F	W	I	S
T	W	P	S	A	S	W	J	I	K	A
R	E	S	T	A	U	R	A	N	T	X
Y	L	G	A	B	T	F	Y	N	K	O
L	L	H	R	N	A	U	L	E	L	P
F	D	S	H	F	L	N	F	R	U	H
D	O	F	X	M	E	N	X	G	N	O
I	N	D	I	A	N	S	I	H	C	N
W	E	L	I	H	T	X	D	J	H	E

b) Write the words in English and German. Schreibe die Wörter auf Englisch und Deutsch auf.

_____   _____

_____   _____

_____   _____

_____   _____

_____   _____

What's the word?

1. Nach dem Mittagessen spiele ich Korbball.

   _____ lunch I play _____ .

2. Meine Mannschaft ist toll.

   My _____ is great.

3. Ich liebe Korbball. Es ist toll zu gewinnen.

   I _____ netball. It's great to _____ .

4. Wir gewinnen viel.

   We win _____ .

5. In meiner Freizeit mache ich Musik.

   In my _____ I play music.

6. Mittwochs habe ich Musikprobe.

   _____ I have music

   _____ .

7. Ich will eine gute Sängerin sein.

   I _____ be a good singer.

8. Elton John ist sehr berühmt.

   Elton John is very _____ .

1 Put in the right words. Setze die richtigen Wörter ein.

`play`   `after`   `Friday`   `Thursday`   `see you`   `netball practice`   `on Wednesdays`

Luke: Let's _____ football on Wednesday.

Dave: No. _____ I have _____ . Are you at home on Thursday?

Luke: No, sorry. On _____ I play tennis with Holly. Friday?

Dave: OK, _____ is good. Let's play _____ lunch.

Luke: OK, _____ .

2 Find the words. Write the English and German words.
Finde die Wörter. Schreibe sie auf Englisch und Deutsch auf.

famouswantteamnetballafterfreetimepracticelove

_____   _____

_____   _____

_____   _____

_____   _____

What's the word?

1. Ich gehe in der Mittagspause nach Hause.

I go home at _____ .

2. Nach dem Mittagessen renne ich mit meinem Hund.

After lunch I _____ with my dog.

3. Ich renne viel herum.

I _____ a lot.

4. Ich bin der Kapitän meines Korbballteams.

I'm the _____ of my netball team.

5. Mittwochs gehen wir in unserer Freizeit ins Tierheim.

On Wednesdays we go to _____

_____ in our free time.

6. Wir lieben es, den Tieren dort zu helfen.

We love to _____ the animals there.

7. Wir helfen jede Woche.

We help _____ week.

3 Match the sentence parts. Ordne die Satzteile zu.

1. I sing and dance
2. I play football with
3. I run with my dog
4. I sing songs in the recording
5. I buy new jeans with my
6. I go to netball
7. I eat at the
8. I talk to my

a) Luke on Fridays.
b) mother on Saturdays.
c) practice on Tuesdays.
d) on Sundays.
e) Sherlock every day.
f) cafeteria on Thursdays.
g) tutor on Mondays.
h) studio on Wednesdays.

4 Complete the words. Vervollständige die Wörter mit den fehlenden Buchstaben und übersetze sie ins Deutsche.

A A A A E E E E E E E E I I I

O U U U U Y

1. __v__r__ _____
2. c__pt___n _____
3. r__n __r___nd _____
4. l__ncht__m__ _____
5. h__lp _____
6. fr___ t__m__ _____
7. t___m _____
8. r__n _____

Yummy!

What's the word?

1. Wir haben eine Cafeteria in der Schule.

   We have a cafeteria _____ school.

2. Am Wochenende haben wir keine Schule. Das ist toll.

   _____ we don't have school. That's great.

3. Ich gehe mit meinen Freunden jeden Monat ins Kino.

   I go to the _____ with my friends every _____ .

4. Dort sehen wir uns Filme an.

   We _____ there.

5. Zu Hause sehe ich viel fern.

   I _____ a lot at home.

6. Ich mag die Sendungen mit Sängern.

   I like the _____ with singers.

7. Ich mag auch Science-Fiction.

   I like _____ too.

5 Cross the odd one out. Ein Wort ist falsch. Streiche es durch.

1. I like
   - TV.
   - month.
   - science fiction.

2. I see my friends at
   - science fiction.
   - school.
   - the weekend.

3. We watch
   - movies.
   - TV.
   - songs.

4. It's time for my favourite
   - programme.
   - recording studio.
   - show.

6 Make sentences. Bilde Sätze über deine Aktivitäten.

- I watch
- I buy
- I play
- I sing
- I eat
- I go
- I read

- every day.
- at the weekend.
- on Mondays.
- on . . .

_____

_____

_____

What's the word?

1. Wir gehen gerne in den Zoo.

We like to go to the _____ .

2. Die Elefanten sind toll.

The _____ are great.

3. Sie kommen aus Indien.

They _____ from _____ .

4. Sie haben auch Pferde aus Deutschland.

They have _____ from Germany too.

5. Die Affen sind lustig.

The _____ are funny.

6. Die Tiger sind neben den Affen.

The _____ are next to the monkeys.

7. Sie haben fünf Bären im Zoo.

They have five _____ at the zoo.

8. Schau, und da ist eine grüne Schlange.

Look, and there's a green _____ .

7 Write the words. Finde die Wörter und schreibe sie auf Englisch und Deutsch auf.

1. myneok _____

2. ozo _____

3. eaehtlnp _____

4. ndlia _____

5. osehr _____

6. gteri _____

7. seakn _____

8. erab _____

8 Make sentences about animals you like. Schreibe auf, welche Tiere du magst und welche nicht.

Beginne mit

I like / I don't like ... _____

_____

_____

_____

_____

_____

What's the word?

1. Es gibt noch mehr Tiere im Zoo.
   Die Papageien sind rot, grün, gelb und blau.

   There are more animals in the zoo.
   The _____ are red, green, yellow and blue.

2. Sie sind elf Jahre alt.

   They are eleven _____ .

3. Papageien sind Vögel.

   _____ are _____ .

4. Die Giraffen sind sehr groß.

   The _____ are very _____ .

5. Sie sind fünf Meter groß.

   They are five _____ .

6. Die Pinguine sind schwarz und weiß.

   The _____ are black and white.

7. Schlangen essen Mäuse.

   _____ eat _____ .

8. Schau, da ist ein Bär mit einem Fisch.

   Look, there's a bear with a _____ .

9. Meine Maus ist zwei Jahre alt.

   My _____ is two years old.

9 **Put the animals in the right box.** Ordne die Tiere dem richtigen Kasten zu.
Einige Tiere können auch auf beiden Seiten stehen.

bat   cat   dog   fish   elephant   penguin   horse   tiger

bear   bird   giraffe   monkey   snake   parrot   mouse

Zoo	Germany
_____	_____
_____	_____
_____	_____
_____	_____
_____	_____
_____	_____
_____	_____

10 **Write the words.** Schreibe die Mehrzahl auf.

one tiger – two _____

one mouse – two _____

one monkey – three _____

one fish – five _____

What's the word?

1. Ich bin zwölf Jahre alt.

    I'm _____ years old.

2. Mein Vater ist fünfundvierzig Jahre alt.

    My father is _____ years old.

3. Meine Großmutter ist achtundsiebzig Jahre alt.

    My grandmother is _____ years old.

4. Mein Onkel ist dreiundfünfzig Jahre alt.

    My uncle is _____ years old.

5. Meine Schwester ist siebzehn Jahre alt.

    My sister is _____ years old.

6. Unser Haus ist die Nummer neunundneunzig.

    Our house is number _____ .

7. Es gibt fünfzehn Spieler in unserer Korbballmannschaft.

    There are _____ players in our netball team.

8. Es gibt einhundert Lehrer an unserer Schule.

    There are _____ teachers at our school.

11 Circle the numbers and write the words.

a) Find the numbers and put a circle around them. Finde die Zahlen und kreise sie ein.

12	13	93	99	16	76	10	37	95
88	64	99	45	83	17	25	64	21
59	22	45	12	76	51	21	69	59
11	12	85	32	81	55	22	14	33
37	77	39	51	34	66	22	21	85
43	37	38	12	33	45	71	62	51
21	20	33	67	81	18	33	35	77
85	14	77	12	13	15	22	22	43
25	43	46	16	14	31	59	99	38

1. eighteen
2. thirty-two
3. ninety-five
4. forty-six
5. twenty
6. thirty-four
7. eighty-three
8. eleven
9. ten
10. fifteen
11. fifty-five
12. sixty-nine
13. thirty-one
14. eighty-eight
15. sixty-seven

b) Write the blue numbers in words. Schreibe die blauen Zahlen als Wörter auf.

_____   _____

_____   _____

What's the word?

1. Lass uns über Essen sprechen. Ich liebe Obst. Und du?

   Let's talk about food. I love _____ . And you?

2. Tiger essen gern Fleisch.

   Tigers like to eat _____ .

3. Ein Tiger isst 7 Kilogramm täglich.

   A tiger eats _____ .

4. Pferde essen Gras.

   Horses eat _____ .

5. Elefanten essen auch Gras.

   Elephants _____ eat _____ .

6. Affen lieben Bananen.

   Monkeys love _____ .

7.

   _____

8.

   _____

---

12 **What do the animals eat? Write the words.** Schreibe auf, was die Tiere essen.

_____ _____ _____ _____

_____ _____ _____

13 **Complete the words.** Vervollständige die Wörter mit den fehlenden Buchstaben und übersetze sie ins Deutsche.

1. m _ _ t _____   `A` `A` `A`

2. pl _ _ nt _____   `A` `A` `A`

3. _ ls _ _____   `A` `E` `E`

4. b _ n _ n _ _ _____   `I` `O` `U`

5. fr _ _ _ t _____

6. w _ t _ r _____

What's the word?

1.	Ich schlafe gerne.	I like to _____ .
2.	Am Wochenende schlafe ich lang.	At the weekend I sleep _____ .
3.	Edgar schläft vier Stunden täglich.	Edgar sleeps _____ .
4.	Das ist nicht viel.	That isn't _____ .
5.	Ich habe nur eine Schwester.	I _____ have one sister.
6.	Meine Mutter redet nicht über ihr Alter.	My mother doesn't talk about her _____ .
7.	Informationen über Blacky, das Pferd:	_____ about Blacky, the horse:
8.	Es kann 40 Kilometer pro Stunde laufen.	It can run _____ .
9.	Es ist 110 Zentimeter lang.	It is 110 _____ .

14 Put in the right words. Setzte die richtigen Wörter ein.

hour	an	long	much	only	a

1. My ruler is thirty centimetres _____ .

2. They _____ like bananas.

3. He sleeps an _____ a day.

4. We have lessons five days _____ week.

5. I don't eat _____ .

6. Can you run forty kilometres _____ hour?

15 Look at the pictures and write the words in English and German.
Schau dir die Bilder an und schreibe die Wörter auf Englisch und Deutsch auf.

_____

_____

_____

_____

What's the word?

1. Hier ist Lizzys Steckbrief.	Here's Lizzy's _____ .
2. Sie lebt im Zoo.	She _____ in the zoo.
3. Sie isst kleine Tiere.	She eats _____ animals.
4. Sie ist aus Afrika.	She's from _____ .
5. Im Winter schläft sie fünf Monate lang.	In _____ she sleeps _____ _____ .
6. Dann arbeiten die Tierpfleger nicht mit Lizzy.	Then the _____ don't _____ with Lizzy.
7. Lass uns über andere Tiere sprechen.	Let's talk about _____ animals.

16 Find seven words.

a) Find the English words. (↓ and →) Finde die englischen Wörter.

D	Z	A	D	C	E	I
S	O	S	N	A	P	B
W	O	R	K	F	R	S
P	K	E	K	R	O	M
N	E	L	W	I	F	A
B	E	T	I	C	I	L
O	P	N	N	A	L	L
T	E	O	T	H	E	R
E	R	Q	E	L	O	P
N	W	I	R	X	U	C

b) Write the words in English and German. Schreibe die Wörter auf Deutsch und Englisch auf.

_____

_____

_____

_____

_____

_____

_____

What's the word?

1. Luke: Ich stehe um sieben Uhr auf.

   Luke: I _____ at seven _____ .

2. Dave: Das ist früh.

   Dave: That's _____ .

3. Luke: Wann stehst du auf?

   Luke: _____ do you get up?

4. Dave: Um acht. Danach gehe ich in die Schule.

   Dave: At eight. _____ I go to school.

5. Luke: Ich frühstücke zuerst.

   Luke: _____ I _____ .

6. Danach füttere ich meinen Hund.

   After that I _____ my dog.

7. Dave: Warum putzt du deine Schuhe?

   Dave: _____ do you _____ your shoes?

8. Luke: Sie sind schmutzig. Es ist Zeit zu gehen.

   Luke: They are _____ . It's time to go.

9. Dave: Lass uns jetzt zu Mittag essen.

   Dave: Let's _____ now.

17 Look at the pictures and write the words. Schau dir die Bilder an und schreibe die Wörter auf.

 I _____ at eight o'clock. First I eat a  _____ .

 After that I _____ to the bathroom. Then I _____

my _____ . She sleeps in my _____ . She loves to

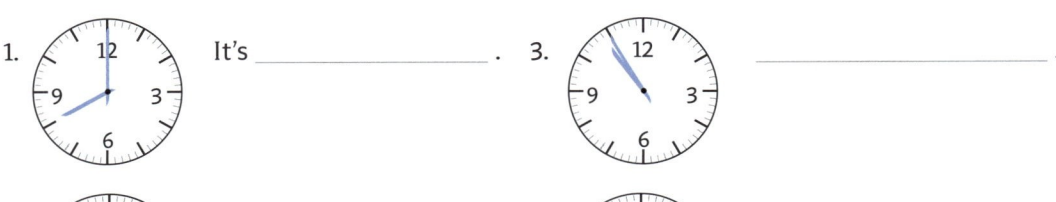 _____ with me. After breakfast I _____ her toilet.

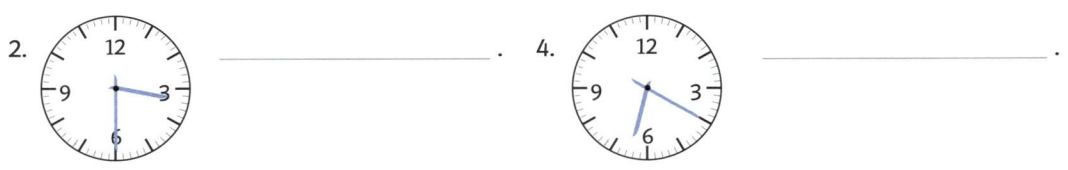 Then I go to _____ . I am at school at nine _____ .

18 What time is it? Write sentences. Wie spät ist es? Schreibe Sätze.

1. It's _____ .

2. _____ .

3. _____ .

4. _____ .

3

What's the word?

1. Ich befrage meinen Mathelehrer.

I _____ my Maths teacher.

2. Es ist ein ausgefüllter Tag.

It's _____ .

3. Du kannst es in der Schulzeitschrift lesen.

You can read it in the school _____ .

4. Wir sprechen über Papas Arbeit.

We talk about dad's _____ .

5. Jeden Montagnachmittag ist er an der Schule.

Every Monday _____ he's at school.

6. Die Lehrer haben ihr Zimmer neben der Cafeteria.

The teachers have _____ room next to the cafeteria.

7.

_____

8. Wie spät ist es?

_____ ?

9. Es ist fünf Uhr. Lass uns Tee trinken.

It's five o'clock. Let's have _____ .

19 Find the words. Write the English and German words.

Finde die Wörter. Schreibe sie auf Englisch und Deutsch auf.

profilecagebreakfastmagazineafternoonearlyworkcleaninterviewo'clockwhyfirst

_____   _____

_____   _____

_____   _____

_____   _____

_____   _____

_____   _____

20 Make sentences. Schreibe auf, was du jeden Tag machst.

I clean the kitchen every day. _____

_____

_____

What's the word?

1. Lasst uns am Samstag in das Café gehen.

   Let's go to the _____ on Saturday.

2. Okay. Danach möchte ich den Hund ausführen.

   OK. After that I want to _____ _____ .

3. Wie alt ist dein Hund?

   _____ old is your dog?

4. Ich weiß es nicht.

   _____ .

5. Er mag Nüsse.

   He likes _____ .

6. Und er ist der schnellste Hund im Park.

   And he is _____ dog in the park.

7. Ich mag die Geschichte nicht.

   I don't like the _____ .

8. Der Polizeibeamte findet einen Hinweis.

   The _____ finds a _____ .

9. Da sind Waschbären in dem Loch.

   There are _____ in the _____ .

21 Right or wrong?

a) Look at the pictures on page 63. Are the sentences right or wrong? Tick ✔ the right box.
Schau dir die Bilder auf Seite 63 im Buch an. Sind die Sätze richtig oder falsch? Kreuze ✔ an.

	right	wrong
1. There is a banana in the café.	☐	☐
2. Mrs Abrihim talks to a police officer.	☐	☐
3. Sherlock looks at the police officer.	☐	☐
4. There is a hole in the ceiling.	☐	☐
5. Luke has a plant in his hands.	☐	☐
6. There is a mess in the café.	☐	☐
7. There is only one box.	☐	☐
8. A raccoon runs in the picture.	☐	☐
9. The chairs are blue.	☐	☐
10. The café's name is Aladin's Park Café.	☐	☐

b) What's not in the story? Underline the words. Unterstreiche alle Wörter, die nicht in der Geschichte vorkommen oder auf keinem Bild auf Seite 63 zu sehen sind.

1. raccoon, birds, dog, snake, bear, fish

2. chair, tables, shelf, boxes, bed

3. boy, girl, man, woman, pet, police officer

4. park, school, café, zoo, playground

What's the word?

1. Lasst uns das <u>Rätsel</u> <u>lösen</u>.

   Let's _____ the _____ .

2. Wir können uns <u>nach</u> Spuren <u>umsehen</u>.

   We can _____ clues.

3. Schaue zur <u>Decke</u>!

   Look at the _____ !

4. Du kannst mich <u>anrufen</u>.

   You can _____ me.

22 Put in the right words.

a) Put in the right words in English and German. Setze die richtigen Wörter auf Englisch und Deutsch ein.

clue   ceiling   raccoon   hole   café   solve   nuts

mess   football   help   look around   police officer   park

1. The noise is a _____ .

2. Sherlock finds a _____ .

3. There are _____ in the café.

4. Then they go to Mrs Abrihim's _____ .

5. Sherlock loves _____ .

6. The café is a _____ .

7. At the café they see the _____ and Mrs Abrihim.

8. They _____ the café for clues.

9. Luke and Sherlock want to _____ Mrs Abrihim.

10. They want to _____ the mystery.

11. He finds a _____ . It's in the _____ .

12. Luke and Sherlock play football in the _____ .

b) Put the sentences in the correct order. Bringe die Sätze in die richtige Reihenfolge.

_____

What's the word?

1. Schau, da ist ein Flamingo im Park.
   Das ist das erste Mal.

   Look, there's a _____ in the park.

   That's the _____ .

2. Wir müssen ihm helfen. Lass uns mit ihm zum Zoo gehen.

   We _____ help it. Let's go to the zoo with it.

3. Jetzt ist es halb acht. Um Viertel nach acht haben wir Mathe.

   Now it's _____ .

   At _____ we have Maths.

4. Dass ist nicht einfach. Aber wir schaffen das.

   That's not easy but _____ .

5. Wie können wir in den Zoo hereinkommen?

   How can we _____ the zoo?

6. Sie öffnen um Viertel vor acht.

   They open at _____ .

7. Dann können wir auch die Löwen und Kamele sehen.

   Then we can see the _____ too.

8. Aber die Krokodile und Zebras können wir nicht sehen. Sie gehen spät ins Bett.

   But we can't see the _____ _____ . They _____ late.

23 Put a circle around the odd one out. Write it in German.

Welches Wort passt nicht in die Reihe? Kreise es ein. Schreibe es auf Deutsch auf.

1. cat • flamingo • dog _____

2. flamingo • parrot • lion _____

3. penguin • fish • zebra _____

4. horse • bat • crocodile _____

5. plant • fruit • tree • camel _____

24 Finish the words. Vervollständige die Wörter.

1. _____ bed (ins Bett gehen)

2. the _____ time (das erste Mal)

3. _____ past (halb)

4. _____ to (müssen)

5. We _____ it! (Wir schaffen das!)

6. _____ to (Viertel vor)

7. quarter _____ (Viertel nach)

8. to _____ in (hereinkommen)

What's the word?

1. Der Oktober ist ein besonderer Monat.

October is a _____ month.

2. Halloween ist im Oktober.

Halloween is _____ .

3. Ich feiere es mit meinen Freunden.

I _____ it with my friends.

4. Wir gehen zu Häusern und sagen: „Süßes, sonst gibts Saures!"

We go to houses and say: " _____ _____ !"

5. Wir tragen Kostüme.

We _____ .

6. Sie sind sehr gruselig.

They are very _____ .

7. Im Februar oder im März tragen wir auch Kostüme.

In _____ or _____ we wear costumes too.

8. Dann tragen wir eine rote Nase.

Then we wear a red _____ .

1 Write the months. Finde die Monate und schreibe sie auf Englisch und Deutsch auf.

1. Jneu _____

2. Stempbere _____

3. ebrFurya _____

4. yJlu _____

5. priAl _____

6. rNovbeem _____

2 Look at the pictures and write the months in English and German.
Schau dir die Bilder an und schreibe die Monate auf Englisch und Deutsch auf.

A _____

O _____

J _____

M _____

D _____

What's the word?

1. Meine Freunde haben kein Geld.

   My friends have no _____ .

2. Meine Freunde und ich gehen zusammen Geld sammeln.

   My friends and I _____ money _____ .

3. Dann tragen wir schöne Kleider und wir sehen sehr unterschiedlich aus.

   Then we wear nice _____ and we look very _____ .

4. Am Abend machen wir ein Feuer.

   In the _____ we make a _____ .

5. Ich bekomme Kleidung und Geld von meiner Familie.

   I _____ clothes and money from my family.

6. Meine Freundin ist eine Muslimin.

   My friend is a _____ .

7. Sie feiert Eid mit ihrer Familie.

   She celebrates _____ with her family.

3 Complete the words. Vervollständige die Wörter mit den fehlenden Buchstaben und übersetze sie ins Deutsche.

A A E E E E E E E E E I I I I I
O O O U

1. c__ll__ct _____
2. cl__th__s _____
3. sp__c___l _____
4. __v__n__ng _____

5. d__ff__r__nt _____
6. f__r__ _____
7. c__st__m__s _____
8. __pr__l _____

4 Find thirteen words.

a) Find the English words. (↓ and →) Finde die englischen Wörter.

F	S	E	P	T	E	M	B	E	R
Y	P	S	D	D	K	M	L	W	M
C	E	L	E	B	R	A	T	E	M
O	C	I	V	V	W	R	U	A	A
S	I	V	E	R	S	C	A	R	Y
T	A	E	N	E	B	H	L	G	X
U	L	A	I	Y	M	O	N	E	Y
M	I	S	N	O	S	E	H	I	L
E	T	O	G	E	T	H	E	R	C

b) **Write the words.** Schreibe die Wörter auf.

_____

_____

_____

_____

What's the word?

1. Im Dezember feiern wir Weihnachten zusammen.

   In _____ we celebrate _____ together.

2. Wir feiern meinen Geburtstag im April.

   We celebrate my _____ in April.

3. Es gibt eine kleine Feier mit meiner Familie.

   There is a small _____ with my family.

4. Und eine große Feier mit meinen Freunden.

   And a _____ party with my friends.

5. Meine Mutter kauft Süßigkeiten.

   My mother buys _____ .

6. An meinem Geburtstag gehe ich spät ins Bett.

   On my birthday I _____ late.

5 Find the words. Write the English and German words.

Finde die Wörter. Schreibe sie auf Englisch und Deutsch auf.

bigAprilsweetsbirthdaychristmasgotobedpartyfire

_____   _____

_____   _____

_____   _____

_____   _____

6 Look at the pictures and write the words in English and German. Schau dir die Bilder an und
schreibe die Wörter auf Englisch und Deutsch auf.

_____

_____

_____

_____

_____

What's the word?

1. Der Geburtstag meiner Mutter ist am achten Februar.

   My mother's birthday is on _____ February.

2. Der Geburtstag meines Vaters ist am elften Mai.

   My father's birthday is on _____ May.

3.

   _____

   _____

4. Im Juli feiere ich meinen zwölften Geburtstag.

   In July I celebrate my _____ birthday.

5. Das ist meine fünfte große Party.

   This is my _____ big party.

6.

   _____ November

7. Das ist meine erste CD.

   This is my _____ CD.

8. Das ist heute mein dritter Film.

   This is my _____ movie today.

7 **Complete the numbers and the sentences.** Vervollständige die Zahlen und die Sätze.

1. 1st   This is Luke's _____ present.

2. 9th   The school is the _____ house on the right.

3. _____ Sam's birthday is on fourth October.

4. _____ We celebrate Christmas on twenty-fourth December.

5. _____ 'M' is the _____ letter of the alphabet.

8 **Look at the pictures and complete the sentences.**
Schaue dir das Bild an. Vervollständige die Sätze zu jeder Person.

inline skates	cap
orange sweatshirt	
skateboard	green
skirt	blue jeans
red clothes	yellow T-shirt
white	black
shoes	orange
football	T-shirt
banana	

1. The first person has _____ jeans.

2. The _____ person has _____ shoes.

3. The _____ person has blue jeans.

4. The _____ boy has _____ shoes and has a _____ in his hand.

5. The fourth person _____ .

6. _____

What's the word?

1. Lasst uns einen Grill kaufen.

   Let's buy a _____ .

2. Wir wollen eine Grillparty machen.

   We want to _____ .

3. Wir haben immer Fleisch.

   We _____ have meat.

4. Und oft haben wir Kuchen.

   And we _____ have cake.

5. Manchmal haben wir auch Obst.

   We _____ have fruit too.

6. Aber wir haben nie Bananen.
   Ich mag sie nicht.

   But we _____ have bananas. I don't like them.

7. Es macht immer viel Spaß.

   It's always a lot of _____ .

9 **Match the word parts.** Ordne die Wortteile zu. Schreibe sie auf Englisch und Deutsch auf.

al	times
par	ten
birth	ty
ne	ways
bar	day
of	ver
some	becue

_____

_____

_____

_____

_____

_____

_____

10 **Complete the words.** Vervollständige die Wörter mit den fehlenden Buchstaben und übersetze sie ins Deutsche.

A A A A E E E E E E E I O O
U U U

1. pr__s__nt _____
2. b__rb__c___ _____
3. f__n _____
4. ch__c__l__t__ _____
5. c__rd _____
6. c__t__ _____
7. c__k__ _____
8. g__v__ _____

What's the word?

1. Es ist Halloween. Lasst uns eine Verkleidungsparty machen.

   It's Halloween. Let's _____ _____ .

2. Die Kostüme sind eine Überraschung.

   The costumes are a _____ .

3. Ich möchte meine Freunde einladen.

   I want to _____ .

4. Lasst uns Karten kaufen.

   Let's buy _____ .

5. Ich möchte sie meinen Freunden geben.

   I want to _____ them to my friends.

6. Ich liebe es, Geschenke zu kaufen.

   I love to buy _____ .

7. Meine Mutter kann einen Kuchen für uns backen.

   My mother can _____ for us.

8. Mein Hund ist auch da. Ich möchte ihm auch ein Kostüm kaufen.

   My dog is there too. I want to buy _____ a costume too.

11 Match the sentence parts. Ordne die Satzteile zu.

1. Dave sometimes has a fancy
2. I want to invite
3. At the weekend we often go
4. My father always makes
5. Jay and Luke like to
6. My family sometimes
7. Holly's birthday is

a) a cake for my birthday.
b) watch movies.
c) on 7th July.
d) my friends.
e) to the cinema.
f) dress party.
g) has a barbecue party.

12 Look at the pictures and write the words. Schau dir die Bilder an und schreibe die Wörter auf.

_____

_____

_____

_____

What's the word?

1. Am Wochenende wollen wir ins Kino gehen.

   At the weekend we want to _____ _____ .

2. Wir schauen gerne Filme.

   We like to _____ .

3. Manchmal sind die Filme schlecht.

   Sometimes the movies are _____ .

4. Wir essen immer Schokolade.

   We always eat _____ .

5.

   _____

6. Mein Hund ist niedlich.

   My dog is _____ .

7. Ich vergesse den Geburtstag meiner Mutter nie.

   I never _____ my mum's birthday.

13 Put a circle around the odd one out. Write it in German.

Welches Wort passt nicht in die Reihe? Kreise es ein. Schreibe es auf Deutsch auf.

1. never • sometimes • often • him   _____

2. fun • forget • get • give   _____

3. nut • barbecue • chocolate • banana   _____

4. present • cake • elephant • card   _____

5. good • nice • great • bad   _____

6. second • third • forget • fifth   _____

7. barbecue • fire • meat • cute   _____

8. surprise • sweet • chocolate • cake   _____

14 Look at the pictures and complete the sentences. Schau dir die Bilder an und vervollständige die Sätze.

1. Dave always gives Holly a _____ .

2. I always _____ all my friends to my birthday party.

3. We often eat _____ at birthday parties.

4. I sometimes _____ with my friends.

5. Or we _____ on TV at home.

What's the word?

1. Ich liebe Einkaufen.

   I love _____ .

2. Wir gehen immer in den Tante-Emma-Laden.

   We always go to the _____ .

3. Wir kaufen dort einige Dinge.

   We buy _____ _____ there.

4. Was kann ich für dich tun?

   _____ ?

5. Wir brauchen Sachen für meinen Geburtstag.

   We _____ things for my birthday.

6.

   _____

7.

   two _____

8.

   _____

9. Darf es sonst noch etwas sein?

   _____ ?

10.

   _____

---

15 Put in the right words. Setzte die richtigen Wörter ein.

| else | can | forget | of | need | some |

Mr Benn: Hello. How _____ I help you?

Dave: I _____ two pencils

and _____ things for my birthday.

Mr Benn: OK, here you are. Anything _____ ?

Dave: Yes, a bar _____ chocolate, please.

I never _____ chocolate!

---

16 Write the words. Finde die Wörter und schreibe sie auf Englisch und Deutsch auf.

1. aeslndc _____

2. rba fo lactecoho _____

3. xbo _____

4. sgtnhi _____

5. eden _____

6. etfrgo _____

What's the word?

1. Lass uns zehn Eier und Zucker kaufen.

   Let's buy ten _____ and _____ .

2. Brauchen wir auch Milch?

   Do we need _____ too?

3. Ich muss auf meinen Einkaufszettel schauen.

   I have to look at my _____ .

4. Nein, aber wir brauchen Schokolade und Butter.

   No, but we need chocolate and _____ .

5. Okay. Ich brauche auch Käse für ein belegtes Brot.

   OK. I need _____ for a _____ too.

6. Lass uns Orangen kaufen.

   Let's buy _____ .

7. Und wir brauchen Chips und Cola für die Party.

   And we need _____ and _____ for the party.

17 **Write a list.** Schreibe die Einkaufsliste für das Rezept auf Englisch.

6 Eier
400g Nüsse
50g Butter
200g Zucker
50ml Milch
1 Tafel Schokolade
1 Banane
Kerzen zur Dekoration

shopping list

18 **Cross the odd ones out.** Streiche die Wörter durch, die nicht zur Party passen.

bad surprise • sandwiches • chocolate • balloon • never • cake • some • candles • crisps •

coke • sweets • sometimes • costumes • friends • fun

What's the word?

1. Wie viel kostet diese Tafel Schokolade?

   _____ this bar of chocolate?

2. Sie kostet 99 Pence.

   It _____ .

3. Ich brauche eine Flasche Cola.

   I need a _____ of coke.

4. Entschuldigung, könntest du das bitte wiederholen?

   _____

   _____ ?

5. Ich brauche auch eine Packung Zucker.

   I need a _____ of sugar too.

6. Wie bitte?

   _____ ?

7. Wir haben keine CDs. Es tut mir leid.

   We don't have _____ . _____ .

8. Ist das alles? Das macht 2 Pfund und 24 Pence.

   That's all? _____ .

9. Hier ist dein Wechselgeld. – Dankeschön.

   _____ . – Thank you.

10. Gern geschehen.

   _____ .

19 Match the sentence parts. Ordne die Satzteile zu.

1. How	a) welcome.
2. Sorry, can you	b) much is the sugar?
3. Anything	c) eggs?
4. Where are the	d) change.
5. You're	e) else?
6. Here's your	f) say that again, please?
7. I need a bar	g) of chocolate.
8. How can I	h) are 99 p.
9. The pencils	i) £5.46.
10. I	j) help you?
11. That's	k) am sorry.

What's the word?

1. Das ist die <u>Einladung</u> für meine Freunde.

   This is the _____ for my friends.

2. <u>Jeder</u> bekommt eine. Ich gebe sie <u>ihnen</u>.

   _____ gets one. I give it

   to _____ .

3. Ich <u>denke</u>, die Einladung ist gut.

   I _____ the invitation is good.

4. Ich <u>frage</u> meine Freunde.

   I _____ my friends.

5. Sie sagen, sie ist <u>toll</u>.

   They say it's _____ .

6. <u>Alles Gute zum Geburtstag!</u>

   _____ !

7. Lasst uns ins Haus <u>hineingehen</u>.

   Let's go _____ the house.

20 Find the words. Write the English and German words.

Finde die Wörter. Schreibe sie auf Englisch und Deutsch auf.

thinkinvitationeveryonehappybirthdaybrilliantintothemask

_____   _____

_____   _____

_____   _____

_____   _____

21 Right or wrong?

Read the text on pages 80/81 in your book. Are the sentences right or wrong? Tick ✔ the right box.

Lies den Text auf Seite 80/81 im Buch. Sind die Sätze richtig oder falsch? Kreuze ✔ an.

	right	wrong
1. There is a birthday party at Jay's house.	☐	☐
2. There are nine people at the party.	☐	☐
3. Luke is the pirate.	☐	☐
4. Jay's mum wants to take a photo.	☐	☐
5. There is water on the table.	☐	☐
6. Dave's costume is green.	☐	☐
7. Olivia comes to the party late.	☐	☐
8. Olivia and Jay dance.	☐	☐

What's the word?

1. Ich liebe Karneval.

I love _____ .

2.

_____

3. Luke ist der beste Tänzer.

Luke is the best _____ .

4.

_____

5. Ich möchte ein Foto machen.

I want to _____ .

6.

_____

7. Schlümpfe sind blau und weiß.

_____ are blue and white.

8.

_____

9. Ich bin eine Hexe. Sei vorsichtig!

I'm a witch. _____ !

22 Write the word pairs. Schreibe die Wortpaare auf.

| ask | invitation | them | think | everyone | brilliant |

1. all   – _____
2. ❓   – _____
3. great   – _____

4. party   – _____
5. 💭   – _____
6. they   – _____

23 Find six costumes.

a) Find the English words. (↓ and →) Finde die englischen Wörter.

N	D	C	D	N	U	X	A
P	I	R	A	T	E	V	L
F	S	Y	N	R	W	O	I
C	M	T	C	B	H	P	E
S	U	P	E	R	M	A	N
L	R	N	R	J	K	L	U
M	F	T	W	I	T	C	H

b) Write the words in English and German. Schreibe die Wörter auf Deutsch und Englisch auf.

_____   _____

_____   _____

_____   _____

What's the word?

1. Lieber Luke, …   _____ Luke, …

2.   _____

3. Meine Übernachtungsparty ist am Samstag.   My _____ is on Saturday.

4. Es gibt verschiedene Snacks.   There are different _____ .

5. Es gibt viele verschiedene Nachspeisen.   There are _____ different _____ .

6. Meine Freunde mögen den Kuchen am   My friends _____ the cake _____ .
   liebsten.

7. Wir singen auch Karaoke auf der Party.   We sing _____ at the party too.

24 Put in the missing words. Setze die fehlenden Wörter ein.

D_____ Holly,

This is an i_____ to my s_____ . It's next Saturday.

We want to sing k_____ and we always eat l_____ different sn_____ .

Do you know carrot pudding?

It's a d_____ . I like it b_____ .

See you, Luke

25 Match the words. Ordne die passenden Wörter richtig zu.

1. brilliant   a) carrot pudding
2. say   b) box
3. dessert   c) great
4. snack   d) 3rd
5. invitation   e) ask
6. barbecue   f) sandwich
7. third   g) 100th
8. hundredth   h) 2nd
9. second   i) meat
10. packet   j) card

What's the word?

1. Es ist Samstag. Lasst uns ein Picknick im Park machen.

   It's Saturday. Let's _____ _____ .

2. Nein, ich möchte in einen Freizeitpark gehen.

   No, I want _____ _____ .

3. Okay. Lasst uns zuerst in ein Fastfood-Restaurant gehen.

   OK. Let's _____ _____ first.

4. Dort will ich mein Lieblingsessen genießen.

   I want to _____ _____ there.

5. Ich mag Hamburger am liebsten.

   I like _____ best.

6. Und ich mag Eis mit Erdbeeren.

   And I like _____ with _____ .

7. Jay möchte eine Übernachtungsparty machen.

   Jay wants to _____ .

26 **Translate the words and talk about you.** Übersetze die Wörter und erzähle über dich. Setze die passenden Wörter ein.

| never | sometimes | often | always |

sonntags • Filme schauen

<u>On Sundays I often watch movies.</u> _____

1. im Januar • ein Picknick im Park machen.

   _____

2. an Wochenenden • in einen Freizeitpark gehen

   _____

3. in der Cafeteria • ein Lieblingsessen genießen

   _____

4. mit meinen Freunden • in ein Fastfood-Restaurant gehen

   _____

5. mittwochs • eine Übernachtungsparty machen

   _____

4 Blue words

What's the word?

1. Lass uns einkaufen gehen. Wir brauchen Pfirsiche und Limonade.

   Let's go shopping. We need _____ and _____ .

2. Okay. Lass uns die Dose nehmen.

   OK. Let's take the _____ .

3. Wir brauchen Mehl für den Kuchen.

   We need _____ for the cake.

4.

   _____

5.

   _____

6. Die anderen und ich sind auf einer Verkleidungsparty.

   _____ and I are at a fancy dress party.

7. Ich bin ein Außerirdischer. Hast du Angst?

   I'm an alien. _____ you _____ ?

8. Natürlich habe ich keine Angst.

   _____ I'm not scared.

9.

   _____

10. Dave läutet die Türklingel, aber niemand hört es.

    Dave _____ the _____ , but no one _____ it.

11. Der Erzähler der Geschichte ist ein Junge.

    The _____ of the story is a boy.

27 Put a circle around the odd one out. Write it in German.

Welches Wort passt nicht in die Reihe? Kreise es ein. Schreibe es auf Deutsch auf.

1. peach • orange • strawberry • pasta _____

2. biscuit • coke • lemonade • milk _____

3. sugar • burger • flour • butter _____

4. ice cream • cake • peach • chocolate _____

28 Write the words. Finde die Wörter und schreibe sie auf Englisch und Deutsch auf.

1. lobolerd _____

2. eb radsce _____

3. necad _____

4. nirg _____

5. teh sohert _____

6. reha _____

What's the word?

1. Unsere Wohnung hat zwei Schlafzimmer.

   Our _____ has two bedrooms.

2. Wohnen deine Freunde in deiner Straße?

   Do your friends live in your _____ ?

3. Wir haben ein Haus mit einem Garten.

   We have a _____ with a garden.

4. Samstags spielen wir Fußball im Park.

   On Saturdays we play football in the _____ .

5. Die *Cutty Sark* ist ein berühmtes Schiff.

   The *Cutty Sark* is a famous _____ .

6. Redditch ist eine schöne Stadt.

   Redditch is a nice _____ .

7. Wir haben ein Schwimmbad an unserer Schule.

   We have a _____ at our school.

8. Lass uns ein Sandwich im Café essen.

   Let's have a sandwich in the _____ .

1 Look at the picture and write the words. Schau dir das Bild an und schreibe die Wörter auf.

6 It's a nice _____ .

| 1 | _____ | 3 | _____ | 5 | _____ | 8 | _____ |
| 2 | _____ | 4 | _____ | 7 | _____ | | |

2 Complete the crossword and find another word.
Vervollständige das Kreuzworträtsel und finde das Lösungswort.

1. Dave lives in a . . . .

2. Pirates live on a . . . .

3. Buses go on . . . .

4. There's a playground in Greenwich . . . .

5. I love our swimming . . . .

6. Luke and Holly live in . . . .

7. Greenwich is a famous old . . . .

8. . . . is the eighth month of the year.

What's the word? _____

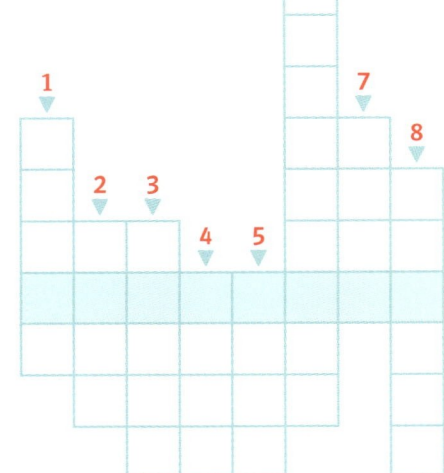

What's the word?

1. Was können wir in diesem <u>Laden</u> kaufen?

   What can we buy in this _____ ?

2. ⟷ <u>new</u>

   The *Cutty Sark* is an _____ ship.

3. Man kann Fußbälle im <u>Sportgeschäft</u> kaufen.

   You can buy footballs in a _____ .

4. Wo ist das <u>Postamt</u>?

   Where is the _____ ?

5. Das Postamt ist im <u>Einkaufszentrum</u>.

   The post office is in the _____

   _____ .

6. Ich gehe <u>Sonntag morgens schwimmen</u>.

   I _____ on Sunday mornings.

3 Where can you find the things in the pictures? Schaue dir die Bilder an und schreibe auf, wo man diese Dinge finden kann.

_p_ _ _ _ _ _ _o_ ___ _t_ _ _f_ _ _ _ _h_ _ _ _ _ _ _ _m_ _ _ _ _ _o_

_ _ _ _ _e_ / _ _ _t _ _r_ _t_ _ _ _ _a_ _ _

4 Put in the right words. Setze die richtigen Wörter ein.

| pool | museum | town | house | café | swimming | park |

Luke lives in a _____ in Greenwich. Greenwich is a famous, old _____ in London. It has a big _____ , and Luke often takes his dog, Sherlock, there. There's a _____ about time with some old clocks and a café in the park. Luke often eats a sandwich in the _____ . There's also a swimming _____ in Greenwich, and Luke often goes _____ there with Dave or other friends.

What's the word?

1. Ich frühstücke jeden Morgen.

    I eat breakfast every _____ .

2. Es ist Montag. Gestern war Sonntag.

    It's Monday. _____ was Sunday.

3. Ich bin müde und ich will ins Bett gehen.

    I'm _____ and I want to go to bed.

4. Luke: Fußball ist immer spannend.

    Luke: Football is always _____ .

5. Weißt du was? Heute habe ich Geburtstag.

    _____ ? It's my birthday.

6. Gefallen dir meine neuen Turnschuhe?

    Do you like my new _____ ?

7. Letzte Woche kam ein guter Film im Fernsehen.

    There was a good film on TV _____ week.

8.

    I love _____ .

9. Ich mache meine Hausaufgaben in der Küche.

    I _____ my _____ in the kitchen.

10. Ich bin jetzt sehr glücklich.

    I'm very _____ now.

5 Complete the Crossword.

a) Complete the crossword. Vervollständige das Kreuzworträtsel.

Down ▼ :
1. There's a ... pool in Greenwich.
2. You need these for sport.
4. It's 15th August now. ... was the 14th.
6. We often eat ... in the cafeteria at school.

Across ▶ :
3. Why are you ...? – I went to bed late.
5. Some films are very ... .
7. School starts at 9:00 in the ... .
8. 31st December is the ... day of the year.
9. A new phone? I'm really ... for you!

b) Make a word from the letters in the blue boxes. Bilde ein Wort aus den Buchstaben in den blauen Kästchen.

What's the word?
Something you like to drink: _____

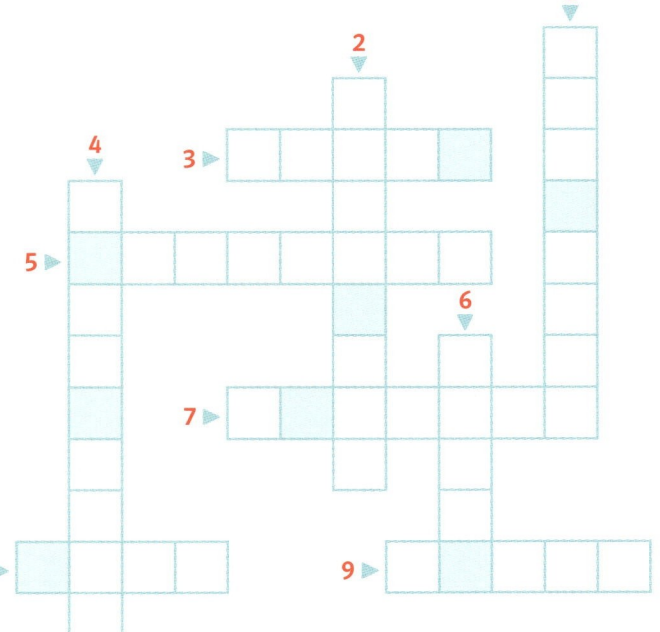

What's the word?

1. Gestern <u>war</u> Daves Geburtstag.

   Yesterday it _____ Dave's birthday.

2. Wir <u>haben</u> das Spiel am Samstag <u>gewonnen</u>.

   We _____ the game on Saturday.

3. Gestern <u>habe</u> ich eine berühmte Person <u>gesehen</u>.

   I _____ a famous person yesterday.

4. Luke <u>hat</u> ein Sandwich in dem Café <u>gekauft</u>.

   Luke _____ a sandwich in the café.

5. Am Montag <u>bist</u> du früh nach Hause <u>gegangen</u>.

   You _____ home early on Monday.

6. Luke <u>hatte</u> gestern Fußballtraining.

   Luke _____ football practice yesterday.

7. Sie <u>haben</u> ihre Hausaufgaben in der Schule <u>gemacht</u>.

   They _____ their homework at school.

8. <u>Erzähl</u> mir bitte eine Geschichte.

   _____ me a story, please.

6 Put in the right verb forms. Setze die richtigen Verbformen ein.

infinitive	simple past	German
to tell		
	was, were	
to have		haben
to buy		
	went	
		sehen
to win		

7 One sentence part is right. Put a circle around it. Kreise die richtigen Satzteile ein.

1. Amina went
   - to the shops.
   - new trainers.
   - happy.

2. Ken bought
   - at the sports shop.
   - a new T-shirt.
   - on Saturday.

3. Sue told me
   - pizza.
   - a story.
   - money.

4. Daniel's party was
   - to a café.
   - a good friend.
   - at his house.

What's the word?

1. Ich fahre mit dem Fahrrad zur Schule.

   I go to school by _____ .

2. Wir fahren immer mit dem Bus in die Stadt.

   We always go to town by _____ .

3. Wir haben ein neues deutsches Auto.

   We have a new German _____ .

4. Mein Onkel hat ein altes Schiff.

   My uncle has an old _____ .

5. Ich gehe gern im Meer schwimmen.

   I like to go swimming in the _____ .

6. Und ich spiele gern Volleyball am Strand.

   And I like to play volleyball on the _____ .

7. Unser Hund liebt es, Frisbee zu spielen.

   Our dog loves to play _____ .

8. Nach dem Ausflug waren wir sehr müde.

   After the trip we _____ very tired.

9. Meine Oma wohnt am Meer.

   My grandma lives _____ .

10. Meine Oma machte einen Ausflug nach London.

    My grandma went on a _____ to London.

11. Es gibt einen Zug von London nach Paris.

    There's a _____ from London to Paris.

12.

    I like to get _____ from friends.

13. Man isst oft Pommes in England.

    You often eat _____ in England.

8 Find eight words.

a) Find the English words. (↓ and →) Finde die englischen Wörter.

C	L	P	L	C	H
B	E	A	C	H	L
Y	T	F	E	X	P
M	R	V	C	A	R
C	A	B	T	C	T
B	I	K	E	H	S
V	N	G	A	I	H
S	E	A	M	P	I
U	N	B	U	S	P

b) Write the words in English and German.
Schreibe die Wörter auf Englisch und Deutsch auf.

_____

_____

_____

_____

_____

_____

_____

_____

What's the word?

1. Wir gehen immer zu Fuß in die Stadt.

   We always go to town _____ .

2. Kann man nach London laufen? – Nein, es ist zwei Stunden von hier entfernt.

   Can you walk to London? – No, _____

   _____ .

3. Wir können mit dem Zug fahren.

   We can go _____ train.

4. London ist groß und ich verirre mich oft dort.

   London is big and I often _____ there.

5. Wir haben uns verirrt. – Oje.

   We got lost. – _____ .

6. Wir finden den Weg mit unserem Navi.

   We find our way with our _____ .

7. Bringe bitte das Buch auf dem Weg nach Hause mit.

   Please get the book _____ home.

8. Es tut mir leid. Ich habe das Buch vergessen.

   Sorry, I _____ the book.

9. Ich bin Vegetarier. Ich esse kein Fleisch.

   I'm a _____ . I don't eat meat.

10. Die Pommes sind kalt. Ich kann sie nicht essen.

    The chips are _____ . I can't eat them.

11. Ich möchte meine Postkarten verschicken.

    I want to _____ my postcards.

9 Find the words and put them in. Finde die Wörter heraus und setze sie ein.

| asseeid | carostpd | dens | prit | slot | morf | yb | antsav |

Ben: We went to my uncle's house last week. He lives at the _____ .

Lizzy: Oh, I didn't get your _____ .

Ben: I didn't _____ you a postcard. We were only there for three days.

Lizzy: Oh, did you have a good _____ ?

Ben: No, we didn't. We got _____ . Margate is only three hours _____ here, but we needed

six hours.

Lizzy: Why didn't you go _____ train?

Ben: My dad wanted to go by car because he has a new _____ .

What's the word?

1. Sie sprechen Englisch in Australien.

   They speak English in _____ .

2. Dieser Mann ist aus Australien.

   This _____ is from Australia.

3. Es gibt schöne Strände in Australien.

   There are _____ beaches in Australia.

4.

   Don't go swimming with a _____ .

5. Ich mag Haie nicht. Sie sind furchtbar.

   I don't like sharks. They are _____ .

6. Ich bin sehr hungrig. Ich will Kartoffeln essen.

   I'm very _____ . I want to eat _____ .

7. Dann lass uns heute einen Sack Kartoffeln kaufen.

   Then let's buy a _____ of potatoes _____ .

8. Wir haben Kisten auf dem Dachboden.

   We have boxes in our _____ .

9. Mein altes Tagebuch ist auch auf dem Dachboden.

   My old _____ is in the attic too.

10.

    _____ eat grass.

11. Man bekommt Wolle von Schafen.

    You get _____ from sheep.

12. Meine Großeltern hatten ein interessantes Leben, aber mein Leben ist langweilig!

    My grandparents had interesting _____ , but my _____ is boring!

10 Match the word pairs. Ordne die Wortpaare richtig zu

1. potatoes	a) yesterday	
2. today	b) he	
3. sheep	c) nice	
4. man	d) food	
5. beautiful	e) wool	
6. bag	f) water	
7. diary	g) box	
8. shark	h) potatoes	
9. attic	i) write	

What's the word?

1. Ist deine Mutter zuhause? – Nein, sie ist heute unterwegs.

   Is your mum at home? – No, she's _____ _____ today.

2. Ich esse immer Popcorn im Kino.

   I always eat _____ in the cinema.

3. Entschuldigung, ist hier in der Nähe ein Postamt?

   _____, is there a post office near here?

4. Dein Fahrrad ist fertig. – Oh gut. Aber kann ich später nochmal wiederkommen?

   Your bike is ready. – Oh good. But _____ _____ ?

5. Klar! Wann kannst du kommen?

   _____ ! What time can you come?

11 Where are they?

a) Match the sentence parts. Ordne die Satzteile zu.

1. Can I come
2. Excuse
3. He's out and
4. That's
5. But that's two hours
6. Guess
7. He's on

a) from here.
b) his way here.
c) back for it later?
d) what?
e) about in Margate.
f) at the seaside.
g) me.

b) Complete the text with the sentences from above. You don't need one of them.
Vervollständige den Text mit den Sätzen von oben. Ein Satz bleibt übrig.

A. At school

Student's dad: _____ . Where's Mr Potter, please?

English teacher: The Geography teacher? _____ .

Student's dad: Margate? _____ .

English teacher: Yes, that's right. He's on a school trip with class 7a.

Student's dad: _____ .

English teacher: Yes, two hours by car. But it's only an hour from here by train.

B. At the music shop

Lucy: _____ ? Ray-B's in town.

George: Who's he?

Lucy: Ah, you know. He's a famous singer. _____ .

What's the word?

1. _____ into Crane Street.

2. Kannst du mir bitte sagen, wie man zum Strand kommt?
   _____
   the beach, please?

3. Gehe geradeaus und biege links ab.
   Walk _____ and _____ .

4. Das Krankenhaus ist auf der linken Seite.
   The hospital is _____ .

5. Gehe geradeaus und das Café ist auf der rechten Seite.
   Go straight on and the café is _____ .

6. Das Postamt ist gegenüber von dem Laden.
   The post office is _____ the shop.

7. Unser Haus ist am Ende der Straße.
   Our house is _____ .

12 Look at the pictures and complete the sentences. Schaue dir die Bilder an und vervollständige die Sätze.

1

Walk straight _____ and _____ into London Road.

4

The post office is _____ .

2

The swimming pool is _____ _____ .

5

The sports shop is _____ the cinema.

3

Walk _____ on and the corner shop is _____ !

6

_____ to the beach, please? – Yes, _____ into Margate Road and the beach is _____ _____ .

What's the word?

1. Nach dem Weg fragen ist nicht immer leicht.

   _____ isn't always easy.

2. Viele Touristen besuchen Margate jedes Jahr.

   Lots of _____ visit Margate every year.

3. Wo ist die Touristeninformation, bitte?

   Where's the _____ , please?

4. Ich laufe gern am Strand entlang.

   I love to walk _____ the beach.

5. Mein Vater arbeitet in einem Krankenhaus.

   My dad works in a _____ .

6. Meine Mama arbeitet bis 8 Uhr.

   My mum works _____ 8 o'clock.

13 Put a circle around the odd one out. Write it in German. Welches Wort passt nicht in die Reihe? Kreise es ein. Schreibe es auf Deutsch auf.

1. opposite • hospital • along • left   _____

2. man • tourist • ship • child   _____

3. asking the way • Tourist information Centre • post office • swimming pool   _____

4. on the left • on the right • out and about • opposite   _____

5. hungry • awful • beautiful • until   _____

14 Complete the sentences. Start at "You are here". Schau dir die Karte an und vervollständige die Sätze. Starte am Punkt „You are here".

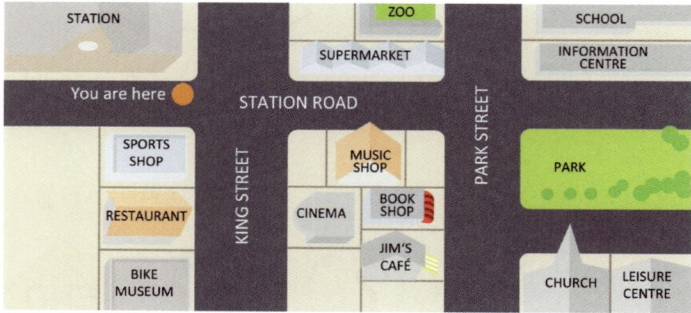

Tourist 1: Can you _____ to the cinema, please?

Henry: Sure. _____ into King Street and it's _____ . It's _____ the restaurant.

Tourist 2: _____ me. _____ to the zoo, please?

Henry: Yes. Go _____ Station Road and then _____ into Park Street. It's _____ and it's _____ the school.

What's the word?

1. In der <u>Bücherei</u> findet man viele Bücher.

   You can find lots of books at the _____ .

2. Im <u>Kaufhaus</u> kann man viele verschiedene Sachen kaufen.

   At the _____ you can buy lots of different things.

3. Wir kaufen immer Obst und Käse auf dem <u>Markt</u>.

   We always buy fruit and cheese at the _____ .

4. Es gibt ein <u>Museum</u> über Schiffe in London.

   There's a _____ about ships in London.

5. Gehe nicht im <u>Fluss</u> schwimmen. Er ist sehr kalt.

   Don't go swimming in the _____ . It's very cold.

6. Ich muss um 5 Uhr am <u>Bahnhof</u> sein.

   I must be at the _____ at 5 o'clock.

7. Meine Eltern fahren mit dem Auto zum <u>Supermarkt</u>.

   My parents go to the _____ by car.

15 Read the dialogues and write the places.

Lies die Dialoge und schreibe auf, wo sich die Personen befinden.

They are …

Mrs Smith:	Excuse me. Where is the sugar, please?	_____
Mr Johnson:	It's on a shelf at the back of the shop. I can show you if you like.	_____
Tina:	Oh, no! We're late. The train goes in five minutes. Excuse me. Where does the train to London go from?	_____
Sam:	It's just over there. You have lots of time.	_____
Ms Adams:	Can I help you?	_____
Luke:	Yes. Can you tell me where the T-shirts are?	_____
Ms Adams:	Yes, of course. They're there – just behind the shoes.	
Mr Baker:	Can I take these books home, please?	
Ms Evans:	Do you have your card?	
Mr Baker:	Er … no.	_____
Ms Evans:	Then I'm sorry. You can look at them here, but you can't take them with you.	_____
Mrs Miller:	I never buy fruit in a supermarket. It's much better here.	_____
Sally:	Yes, but Mum, it's cold here.	_____

What's the word?

1. U-Boote fahren im Meer.

   _____ go under the sea.

2. Eine Straßenbahn ist ein Zug. Sie fährt auf der Straße.

   A _____ is a train. It goes on the road.

3. Menschen fliegen mit dem Flugzeug nach Australien.

   People go to Australia by _____ .

4. Ein Schiff ist ein großes Boot.

   A ship is a big _____ .

5. Hubschrauber bringen Menschen ins Krankenhaus.

   _____ take people to hospital.

6. Mein Vater hat ein Motorrad.

   My dad has a _____ .

7. Die Londoner U-Bahn ist sehr alt.

   The _____ in London is very old.

8. Möchtest du nach London fahren?

   _____ to go to London?

9. Ich möchte jetzt gern ein Eis essen.

   _____ eat an ice cream now.

10. Ich mag mein [skateboard] .

    I like my _____ .

16 Look at the pictures and write the words. Schau dir die Bilder an und schreibe die Wörter auf.

_____   _____   _____   _____

_____   _____   _____   _____

17 Find the words. Write the English and German words.
Finde die Wörter. Schreibe sie auf Englisch und Deutsch auf.

skateboardwouldyoulikeundergroundI'dliketotramplane

_____   _____

_____   _____

_____   _____

What's the word?

1. Wir hatten gestern abend ein tolles Abenteuer.

We had a great _____ last night.

2. Mein Ururopa war berühmt.

My _____ was famous.

3. Mein Bruder hat einen Job in einem Laden.

My brother has a _____ in a shop.

4. ⟷ love

I _____ homework!

5. Meine Schwester übergibt sich oft im Auto.

My sister _____ often _____ in the car.

6. Mein Onkel war letztes Jahr erster Offizier, aber jetzt ist er Kapitän.

My uncle was _____ last year but now he's the captain.

7. Der Sturm gestern Nacht war sehr schlimm.

The _____ last night was very bad.

8. Wellen sind in einem Sturm immer sehr hoch.

_____ are always very high in a storm.

18 **Put a circle around the odd one out. Write it in German.** Welches Wort passt nicht in die Reihe? Kreise es ein. Schreibe es auf Deutsch auf.

1. first mate • great-great-granddad • captain _____

2. hate • love • like _____

3. storm • waves • job _____

19 **Complete the crossword.** Vervollständige das Kreuzworträtsel.

Across ▶ :

1. You can put things in a … .

3. Some people write in a … every day.

5. I really don't like fish – I … it.

6. We love to play in the … in the sea.

7. My sister is always … in the car.

9. I want … and fish for dinner.

10. My uncle isn't the captain, but he's the … .

Down ▼ :

2. My bedroom is under the … .

4. An … story is always exciting.

8. There's a lot of wind. It's a … .

What's the word?

1. Hast du den Schrei gehört? Did you hear that _____ ?

2. „Hilfe! Hilfe! Mann über Bord!" "Help! Help! _____ !"

3. Man braucht viele Seile auf Schiffen. You need a lot of _____ on ships.

4. Ich bin hungrig, deshalb will ich jetzt essen. I'm hungry _____ I want to eat now.

5. Ich hatte viele Pommes zum Mittagessen. I had _____ chips for lunch.

20 Put in the right words. Setz die richtigen Wörter ein.

beach	boats	captain	cold	hated	shark
job	life	lived	mate	nose	seaside	shout
sick	so

My great-great-grandad, Sam, _____ more than a hundred years ago. He lived at the _____ ,

and all his family worked on _____ . Sam loved the sea but he was always _____ on a boat.

His father was a _____ , and his brother was the first _____ on a big ship. Sam was the

joke of his family. He was 16 and he needed a job. _____ he started to work on a farm. His family did

not think it was a good _____ , and Sam _____ the jokes they made about him.

His _____ was not easy.

Some years later Sam was on the _____ with his brother's two boys. The water was _____ ,

but the boys went swimming. Then Sam saw a _____ twenty metres from the boys. He didn't have

time to think so he wasn't scared. He ran into the sea and gave a _____ . The shark saw Sam and

went for him. Sam hit (*schlug*) the shark on its _____ and Sam and the two boys were OK.

After that Sam was famous in their town and all the jokes were about the sharks.

21 Write the words. Finde die Wörter und schreibe sie auf Englisch und Deutsch auf.

1. soper _____

2. naM beroovdar _____

3. tusoh _____

4. a tol fo _____

What's the word?

1. Man kann Milch und Eier auf einem Bauernhof kaufen.

   You can buy eggs and milk on a _____ .

2. Einige Bauern wohnen auf Bauernhöfen.

   Some _____ live on farms.

3. Ich bin die Tochter meines Vaters.

   I'm my dad's _____ .

4. Man bekommt Eier von Hühnern.

   You get eggs from _____ .

5. Unser Hund trägt immer ein Halsband.

   Our dog always wears a _____ .

6. Und unsere Schafe haben GPS-Halsbänder.

   And our sheep have _____ collars.

7.

   Farmers have two or three _____ .

8. Wir gehen in den Ferien oft klettern.

   We often go _____ in the holidays.

9. Im Winter kann man im Schwimmbad Kanufahren gehen.

   In the winter you can go _____ in the swimming pool.

1 Complete the crossword. Vervollständige das Kreuzworträtsel.

Across ▶ :

1. A … is like a car. You see it on a farm.

4. Rock … is a sport.

7. A … is her parents' child.

9. … are animals. You often find them on farms.

Down ▼ :

2. A … is a bird. We eat their eggs.

3. … is a sport on water.

5. Our dog's … has our name on it.

6. A … is a man or woman with a farm.

8. A satnav has … .

What's the word?

1. Man kann Leute im Park <u>kennen lernen</u>.

   You can _____ people in the park.

2. <u>Mach dir</u> darüber keine <u>Sorgen</u>.

   Don't _____ about it.

3. Wir <u>kamen</u> am Sonntag <u>an</u>.

   We _____ here on Sunday.

4. <u>Klicken Sie</u> hier, um einige Fotos zu sehen.

   _____ here to see some photos.

5. Man <u>braucht</u> die Schafe <u>nicht zu</u> füttern. Sie fressen Gras.

   You _____ feed the sheep. They eat grass.

6. <u>Möchtest du</u> unseren Bauernhof sehen?

   _____ to see our farm?

7. <u>Ich möchte</u> Kanufahren.

   _____ go canoeing.

8. <u>Ich möchte nicht</u> klettern gehen.

   _____ go rock climbing.

9. <u>Ich habe</u> die Hühner heute morgen <u>gefüttert</u>.

   I _____ the chickens this morning.

2 Put in the right words. Setze die richtigen Wörter ein.

> tractor   meets   came   like   farmer   canoeing
> wouldn't   fed   needn't

Reporter: Hello. When did you come to Patterson's farm?

A mother: We _____ on Sunday.

Reporter: And do you and your children like it?

A mother: Yes, it's great. We like it, and our daughter loves it here too.

Reporter: Do her friends come here?

A mother: No, but that isn't a problem. She always _____ other children here.

Reporter: What do they do here?

A mother: They feed the animals – this morning they _____ the chickens – or they help with the

   _____ . And they _____ do things on the farm every day. They can go

   _____ or rock climbing.

Reporter: And would you _____ to live on a farm?

A mother: Well, yes. I'd like to live on a farm, but I _____ like to be a _____ .

   They always get up very early and work very late.

What's the word?

1. Ich mag das Land, aber ich mag auch Städte.

   I like the _____ , but I like towns too.

2. Wir gehen oft auf Klassenfahrten.

   We often go on _____ .

3. Im Sommer fahren wir immer in Urlaub.

   We always go on _____ in the summer.

4. Meine Großmutter wohnt auf dem Land.

   My grandmother lives _____ .

5. Unser Haus ist in der Nähe von einem Park.

   Our house is _____ a park.

6. Unsere Schule ist sehr modern.

   Our school is very _____ .

7. Unsere Cousins treffen uns jeden Sommer.

   Our cousins meet _____ every summer.

8. Dieses Spiel ist langweilig.

   This game is _____ .

9. Klettern kann beängstigend sein.

   Rock climbing can be _____ .

3 Read and put in the right words. Lies die Texte und füge das passende Adjektiv ein.

| scary | cold | awful | modern | beautiful | boring |

1. Our house is new and it has new technology in the kitchen and in the bathroom.

   Our house is _____ .

2. He does not like boys and girls, and he hates me too. He is not a nice man.

   He's _____ .

3. I like Alex's picture. He's very good at art. And look at the colours!

   Yes, the picture is _____ .

4. I can't read this book. It isn't funny and it isn't interesting.

   The book is _____ .

5. I like the film. It's very exciting but I can't watch it because I can't sleep after that.

   The film is _____ .

6. It's May. It isn't winter now but I need more clothes. And let's make a fire.

   It's _____ .

4 Match the sentence parts. Ordne die Satzteile zu.

1. I love rock

2. We live in

3. Year 7TM are on

4. I'd like

5. I wouldn't

6. The game is

a) like to live in a town.

b) to have a dog.

c) the country.

d) very boring.

e) a school trip.

f) climbing.

What's the word?

1. Ich habe eine blaue Jacke.

    I have a blue _____ .

2. Wir können keine Jeans in der Schule tragen.

    We can't wear _____ at school.

3. Ich habe drei Schals, aber ich trage nur den Manchester United Schal.

    I have three _____ but I only wear the Manchester United _____ .

4. Ich trage keine Schuhe im Haus.

    I don't wear _____ in the house.

5. Ich habe einen neuen Rock. Magst du ihn?

    I have a new _____ . Do you like it?

6. Wir können weiße oder blaue Socken in der Schule tragen.

    We can wear white or blue _____ at school.

7. Ich liebe dein neues Sweatshirt.

    I love your new _____ .

8. Ich trage Turnschuhe beim Tennis.

    I wear _____ for tennis.

9. Sie mag Äpfel.

    She likes _____ .

10. Ich bin in einer neuen Klasse.

    I'm in a new _____ .

5 **Write the words.** Beschrifte die Kleidungsstücke auf Englisch.

1 _____
2 _____
3 _____
4 _____

5 _____
6 _____
7 _____
8 _____

6 **Answer the questions.** Beantworte die Fragen.

1. It's cold. What do you wear? _____ .

2. What do only girls wear? _____ .

3. What do you wear with socks? _____ .

What's the word?

1. Deine <u>Hose</u> ist schmutzig.

   Your _____ are dirty.

2. Im Sommer trage ich einen Rock und ein <u>T-Shirt</u>.

   In summer I wear a skirt and a _____ .

3. Kann ich dein Handy haben? Ich will ein <u>Telefongespräch</u> führen.

   Can I have your mobile? I want to make a _____
   _____ .

4. <u>Wie geht's dir?</u> – Mir geht's gut, danke.

   _____ ? – I'm fine, thanks.

5. Ich habe lange <u>Arme</u>.

   I have long _____ .

6. Mir war schlecht, aber es geht mir jetzt <u>besser</u>.

   I was sick, but I'm _____ now.

7. Mein Hobby ist <u>Reiten</u>.

   My hobby is _____ .

8. Wir machen oft <u>Picknicks</u> im Sommer.

   We often have _____ in summer.

9. Und wir gehen Kanufahren. Dann tragen wir <u>Helme</u>.

   And we go canoeing. Then we wear
   _____ .

7 **Look at the pictures and finish the sentences.** Schau dir die Bilder an und vervollständige die Sätze.

1. She always wears a _____ .   3. He loves _____ .   5. That's a cool _____ .

2. She wants to make a
   _____ .

4. Our dog likes _____ .   6. We have two _____ .

8 **Write the words.** Finde die Wörter und schreibe sie auf Englisch und Deutsch auf.

1. mars _____   4. urtosser _____

2. kosc _____   5. methel _____

3. retebt _____   6. cincpi _____

What's the word?

1. Was gibt's zum Abendessen?

   What's for _____ ?

2. Wales ist ein kleines Land.

   _____ is a small country.

3. Es ist warm in der Küche.

   It's _____ in the kitchen.

4. Hör damit auf!

   _____ that!

5. Mein Bruder hat gestern mein Fahrrad kaputtgemacht. Er macht immer alles kaputt.

   My brother _____ my bike yesterday.

   He always _____ things.

6. Du musst einen Helm tragen.

   You _____ wear a helmet.

7. Du hast das T-Shirt gestern getragen.

   You _____ that T-shirt yesterday.

9 Find six words.

a) Find the English verbs in the infinitive or simple past. (↓ and →) Finde die englischen Verben im Infinitiv oder in der Vergangenheitsform.

A	C	B	O	S	M	N	T
W	O	R	C	B	E	D	S
E	M	O	P	I	E	E	T
A	E	K	O	E	T	X	O
R	F	E	E	D	N	I	P

b) Put in the rights verbs from a). Setze das richtige Verb aus a) ein.

1. You must _____ your pet every day.

2. Can I _____ my new jeans?

3. Come and _____ my friends!

4. Yesterday I _____ my mobile.

5. Lots of people _____ to our town in August.

6. That noise is awful! Please _____ !

What's the word?

1. Dein Bruder ist freundlich.

   Your brother is _____ .

2. Lass uns nächstes Jahr zurückkommen.

   Let's come _____ next year.

3. Wir haben morgen einen Test.

   We have a _____ tomorrow.

4. Du bist spät! – Es tut mir leid.

   You are late! – _____ .

5. Gestern Nacht haben wir eine Nachtwanderung gemacht.

   We went on a _____ last night.

6. Du spielst gut Fußball, aber ich bin der Beste.

   You're good at football but I'm _____ !

7. Geht's dir gut? – Ja, mir geht's gut.

   Are you OK? – Yes, _____ .

8. Bis bald!

   _____ !

10 Complete the words and write the sentences in German. Vervollständige die Wörter in den Sätzen mit den fehlenden Buchstaben. Übersetze die Sätze ins Deutsche.

| A | A | A | A | A | A | E | E | E | E | E | E | I | I |
| O | O | O | O | O | O | O | O | O | U | U |

1. S___ y___ s___n!

   _____

2. L__t's g__ __n __ n__ght w__lk.

   _____

3. Th__t's my sw___tsh__rt.

   _____

4. Is th__t ph__n__ c__ll f__r m__?

   _____

5. It's y___r s__ck.

   _____

11 Match the questions and answers. Ordne die Fragen und Antworten richtig zu.

1. How are you?

2. You want to go?

3. Would you like to go canoeing?

4. Where do you live?

5. I love it here. Must we go home tomorrow?

6. Hey! Do you have my helmet?

a) – Oh sorry! Here you are!

b) – I'm fine, thanks.

c) – In the country.

d) – Yes, but let's come back next year.

e) – Goodbye. See you soon!

f) – No thanks! That's scary.

What's the word?

1. Wie ist das Wetter heute?   _____ today?

2. Heute ist es <u>bewölkt</u> und grau in Schottland.   It's _____ and grey in Scotland today.

3. Das Meer ist oft <u>kalt</u> um England herum.   The sea is often _____ around England.

4. Es ist immer <u>heiß</u> in Australien.   It's always _____ in Australia.

5. Es <u>regnet</u> viel in Manchester.   It _____ a lot in Manchester.

6. Es ist oft <u>sonnig</u> in London.   It's often _____ in London.

7. Es ist <u>warm</u>. Ich brauche meine Jacke nicht.   It's _____ . I don't need my coat.

8. Deine Schuhe sind <u>nass</u>.   Your shoes are _____ .

9. Es ist nicht kalt, aber es ist <u>windig</u>.   It's not cold but it's _____ .

12 **Look at the pictures and complete the sentences.** Schau dir die Bilder an und vervollständige die Sätze.

 1. It's _____

 3. It's _____

 5. It's _____

 2. It's _____

 4. It's _____

 6. It's _____

13 **Look at the map and complete the sentences.**
Schau dir die Karte und vervollständige die Sätze.

Yesterday the weather wasn't bad in Scotland.

It was very _____ , but it was _____ too.

It wasn't so good in Manchester – it _____ in

the morning and was _____ all day. In Devon

the weather was better – it was _____ but it

was _____ too. In Birmingham it was _____

and grey. The best weather was in London – it was

_____ and _____ .

What's the word?

1. Wir wollen um 11 Uhr eine Nachtwanderung machen.

   We want to _____ at 11 p.m.

2. Nachts ist es dunkel.

   It's _____ at night.

3. Ich habe ein komisches Geräusch gehört.

   I _____ a funny noise.

4. Es hat geregnet und ich wurde nass.

   It rained and I _____ wet.

5. Es war gruselig, weil es dunkel war.

   It was scary _____ it was dark.

6. Wir haben Fisch und Pommes zu Mittag gegessen.

   We _____ fish and chips for lunch.

7. Kannst du mich heute Abend anrufen?

   Can you _____ me this evening?

8. Bitte beantworte die Frage.

   Please _____ the question.

9. Der Urlaub war fantastisch.

   The holiday was _____ .

14 Put in the verbs in the past tense. Setze die Vergangenheitsformen der Verben ein.

`ask` `be` `be` `come` `go` `eat` `get` `hear` `see` `tell` `wear`

Last weekend my family and I _____ for a night walk. It was very cold, so we _____ coats.

At first it was very exciting. But we walked for a long time, and I _____ very tired. I didn't want to walk

back to the farm. My brothers were tired too, but they are 15, and I am only 11. We _____ chocolate, but

I was tired. I wanted to go by bus, but Dad _____ us he had no money. "Can't you help me, Dad?"

I asked. "I'm so tired."

Then we _____ a funny noise. "What was that?" I _____ . "I don't know," answered my dad.

We walked and walked, but we didn't talk. We all listened for the noise. Then we heard it. What was it?

A man? An animal? It _____ scary but I wasn't tired.

We walked fast, and 15 minutes later we _____ back at the farm.

I was the fastest and I was the first. Then I heard the noise and looked behind me. I _____ my dad

with his mobile in his hand. The noise _____ from his mobile. "Dad!" I shouted, "It was you.

Why did you do that? That was not funny." Dad said, "Well, I only helped you! We're at the farm now."

What's the word?

1. Ich lese oft nachts mit einer Taschenlampe.

   I often read at night with a _____ .

2. Devon ist ein schöner Ort in England.

   _____ is a beautiful place in England.

3. Spielst du gern Karten?

   Do you like to play _____ ?

4.

   That's my _____ .

5. Ich schreibe jeden Tag SMS.

   I write _____ every day.

6. Wir schauen Basketball im Fernsehen.

   We watch _____ on TV.

7. Man schreibt „Mit den besten Wünschen" am Ende von Postkarten.

   You write "_____" at the end of postcards.

8. Grüße meine Mutter und meinen Vater von mir.

   _____ my mum and dad.

9. Ich hörte das Telefon rechtzeitig.

   I heard the telephone _____ .

---

15 Complete the crossword. Vervollständige das Kreuzworträtsel.

Across ▶ :

1. It rained. Now I'm ... .
3. People play ... in every country.
4. You can write a text ... on your mobile.
5. I was in ... for the bus – I wasn't late.
7. It was really, really great – it was ... .
10. Our dog loves a night ... too.
11. I don't need an ... clock. I have my mobile.

Down ▼ :

2. You write "Best ..." at the end of a postcard.
4. They play ... a lot in the USA.
6. It's always ... at night.
8. It's dark. I need a ... .
9. It's not cold and it's not hot. – No, it's ... .

What's the word?

1. Gestern fiel ich in den Fluss.

   Yesterday I _____ into the _____ .

2. Es gibt ein Problem mit deinen Hausaufgaben.

   There's a _____ with your homework.

3. Er hat große Füße.

   He has big _____ .

4. Oh, mein Fuß. Er steckt fest.

   Oh, my _____ . It's _____ .

5. Ich kriege ihn nicht aus dem Matsch heraus.

   I can't get it _____ the _____ .

6. Das Foto ist sehr dunkel. Ich sehe sein Gesicht nicht.

   The photo is very dark. I can't see his _____ .

7. Ziehe nicht an meinem Schal!

   Don't _____ my scarf!

8. Ziehe nicht an der Tür. Du musst schieben.

   Don't pull the door. You must _____ .

9. Ich sagte, „Nicht ziehen."

   I _____ , "Don't pull."

---

16 **The boy and his dog. Put in the right words and find another word.**
Trage die richtigen Wörter ein und finde das Lösungswort.

1. The boy has two … and the dog has four.
   They walk on them.
2. The boy has two … and his hands are at the end.
3. The boy has five … on every hand.
4. The dog and the boy have a … .
5. The dog has a big … and the boy has a small … .
6. The boy has two … but the dog only has feet.

What's the word?
The boy's dog is also the boy's … _____ .

---

17 **Find the words and write them in the right table.** Finde zehn Verben in der
Vergangenheitsform und schreibe sie in die richtige Tabellenspalte.

1. ehudsp
2. eta
3. isda
4. tog
5. krebo
6. reow
7. ludelp
8. wanderse
9. rehad
10. petopds

regelmäßig	unregelmäßig

What's the word?

1. Rachel sitzt in einem <u>Rollstuhl</u>, weil sie nicht laufen kann.

   Rachel sits in a _____ because she can't walk.

2. Lass uns schauen, was in der <u>Schatzkiste</u> ist.

   Let's see what's in the _____ .

3. Man benötigt GPS für <u>Geocaching</u>.

   You need GPS for _____ .

4. Es gab keinen <u>Schatz</u> in der Schatzkiste.

   There was no _____ in the cache box.

5. Es ist heute wirklich sonnig. Du musst eine <u>Mütze</u> tragen.

   It's really sunny today. You must wear a _____ .

6. Nur Mädchen tragen <u>Blusen</u>.

   Only girls wear _____ .

7. T-Shirts und Blusen sind <u>Tops</u>.

   T-shirts and blouses are _____ .

8. Bei heißem Wetter trage ich immer eine <u>kurze Hose</u>.

   I always wear _____ in hot weather.

18 Look at the pictures and write the words. Schau dir die Bilder an und schreibe die Wörter auf.

   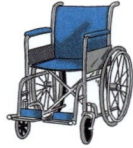

_____   _____   _____   _____

_____   _____   _____   _____

19 Find the words. Write the English and German words.
Finde die Wörter. Schreibe sie auf Englisch und Deutsch auf.

shortsblousewheelchaircapgeocachingtop

_____   _____

_____   _____

_____   _____

What's the word?

1. Das Bild ist sehr bunt.

   That picture is very _____ .

2. Sie ist ein sehr hübsches Mädchen.

   She's a very _____ girl.

3. Es ist neblig. Ich kann nicht viel sehen.

   It's _____ . I can't see very much.

4. Das Wetter ist mild in England. Es ist nicht sehr heiß oder kalt.

   The weather is _____ in England. It isn't very hot or cold.

5. Meine Schuhe waren nass, aber sie sind jetzt trocken.

   My shoes were wet, but they are _____ now.

6. ⟷ warm

   It's _____ today.

7. Seine Kleidung ist immer sehr schick.

   His clothes are always very _____ .

8. John sitzt hinter mir in der Klasse.

   John sits _____ me in class.

9. Er ist zehn Minuten zu spät.

   He's ten _____ late.

20 Write the opposites. Schreibe die Gegenteile auf.

1. into – _____

2. wet – _____

3. warm – _____

4. grey – _____

5. hot – _____

6. exciting – _____

7. cloudy – _____

8. warm – _____

9. left – _____

21 Put a circle around the odd one out. Write it in German. Welches Wort passt nicht in die Reihe? Kreise es ein. Schreibe es auf Deutsch auf.

1. cool • mild • weather • warm _____

2. awful • beautiful • chic • pretty _____

3. foggy • friendly • sunny • windy _____

4. back • behind • opposite • under _____

5. face • minute • finger • foot _____

What's the word?

1. <u>Komm jetzt!</u> Wir sind spät.　　　　　　　　　　_____ ! We're late.

2. <u>Schau</u> das Pferd <u>an!</u> <u>Seine</u> Nase ist blau.　　Look at that horse! _____ nose is blue.

3. Das Schaf <u>steckt</u> im Schlamm fest.　　　　The sheep _____ .

4. Das ist super! <u>Gut gemacht!</u>　　　　　　That's great! _____ !

5. Was können wir jetzt machen? <u>Irgendeine</u>　What can we do now? _____ ?
   <u>Idee?</u>

6. Wo ist mein Handy? – Lass uns <u>danach</u>　　Where's my mobile? – Let's _____ it.
   <u>suchen.</u>

22 Match the words.

a) Match the word parts and write them in German. Ordne die Teile der Wörter richtig zu und schreibe sie auf Deutsch auf.

get	time	_____
come	lost	_____
free	up	_____
get	on	_____
in	of	_____
look	and about	_____
look	time	_____
out	at	_____
out	for	_____

b) Put the words from a) in the sentences. Setzte die Wörter aus a) in die Sätze ein.

1. Oh, no! It's five o'clock. _____ ! We're late.

2. I can't find my coat. Can you _____ it in your house, please?

3. _____ that horse! Isn't it beautiful?

4. Get _____ the sea! There's a shark.

5. Are we _____ for the bus? – Yes, its only quarter to four.

6. What do you do in your _____ ? – Oh, I play basketball.

7. I never see my brother at the weekend. He's always _____ .

8. _____ ! It's eight thirty, and you're in bed.

9. With GPS on my phone I never _____ .

Goodbye